PEOPLE'S POLAND:

Government and Politics

CHANDLER PUBLICATIONS IN
POLITICAL SCIENCE

Victor Jones, *Editor*

PEOPLE'S POLAND:

Government and Politics

Alexander J. Groth

University of California at Davis

CHANDLER PUBLISHING COMPANY
An Intext Publisher
SAN FRANCISCO • SCRANTON • LONDON • TORONTO

Library of Congress Cataloging in Publication Data

Groth, Alexander J   1932-
  People's Poland: government and politics.

  (Chandler publications in political science)
  Bibliography: p.
  1. Poland—Politics and government—1945-
I. Title.
DK443.G75   320.9'438'05   79-172866
ISBN 0-8102-0451-7

To Stevin and Warren

Contents

Preface : : vii

1. Background : : 1

2. The Institutions : : 25

3. The Ruling Party and Its Adjuncts : : 48

4. The Red and the Black: Communism and Catholicism : : 80

5. The Social and Economic Impact of Communist Rule : : 96

6. Foreign Policy : : 118

7. Conclusion : : 136

Bibliographical Essay : : 147

Index : : 151

Preface

THE PURPOSE OF this book is to provide an introduction to the politics of Communist Poland in the 1970s. It is a survey of the background, the major institutions, problems, and personalities of the Polish regime since the Second World War. I hope that it will offer a point of departure for further study not only to those interested in contemporary Poland, but also to students who may want to extend their general knowledge of Communist political systems in Eastern Europe and elsewhere.

All of the so-called Marxist-Leninist regimes are characterized by certain structural and ideological similarities, or "universals", but each regime has its own particular setting and heritage: cultural, economic, geographic. Each is confronted by a different mix of popular traditions, values, and attitudes. Each has its special problems. Thus here, as in most comparative case studies, we balance various general and particular aspects of political life.

The organization of the material is intended to facilitate comparisons and raise questions of interest within several analytical frameworks. Political development, political culture, the distributive impact of Communist power, the interplay of international and domestic politics, all these themes are uniquely reflected in the life history of People's Poland. Under the leadership of Bierut, as of Gomułka and Gierek—facing the Russia of Stalin, Khrushchev, and Brezhnev—Poland has contributed an irrepressibly idiosyncratic personality to the experiment of Communist rule. Thus, within the modest limits of a brief introduction, this volume may be of interest and assistance to all students of comparative politics.

PEOPLE'S POLAND:
Government and Politics

1

Background

THE POLISH STATE which emerged under Communist rule from the Second World War is a striking contrast of continuities and gaps in historical legacy. A realistic appreciation of the contemporary and uniquely Polish brand of Communism requires some attention to both the new and the old elements in the life of modern Poland.

To begin with, there have been profound physical changes since 1939. Geographically, Poland's frontiers have shifted drastically westward. In 1939 about 60 percent of Polish territory lay east of Warsaw; today the reverse is true. As of 1945 Poland had lost 69,290 square miles of her pre-1939 territory to the Soviet Union and gained 39,597 square miles in the west and north at the expense of Germany. The net change has made Poland about one-fifth smaller than she was at the outbreak of the Second World War. * It has also greatly expanded her access to the Baltic from a mere 87 miles to now more than 300. Territorial changes have given the present Polish state much more compact frontiers (only 1,905 miles today as compared with 3,445 in 1939) with a far better transportation network, and the undisputed possession of the Odra and Wisła estuaries, and the major ports of Szczecin, Gdynia, and Gdańsk. On the whole, Poland lost territories of a lower industrial, economic potential, mainly agricultural and forest resources at a fairly primitive level of development, and gained territories with a much higher potential, including mineral resources like coal, a variety of metal ores, particularly lead, zinc, uranium and cadmium, as well as other industrial raw materials. The former German territories of Silesia, Pomerania, and a part of East Prussia incorporated into Poland in 1945 have also added, both in industry and

---

*Poland now has an area of 120,359 sq. mi.

agriculture, much more technologically advanced factories and farms to the Polish economy.

Another significant aspect of Poland's westward shift has been the increased ethnic homogeneity of her population. At least one out of every three inhabitants of prewar Poland was a member of an ethnic minority group. The territories ceded to the USSR were inhabited by several million Ukrainians and Byelorussians who jointly accounted for the largest segment of Polish minority population before 1939 and one which had always presented Polish politicians and administrators in the east with an extremely difficult problem of *modus vivendi*.[1] The new lands in the west were settled by Poles who had been displaced by the Soviets from the former Polish eastern territories. The Germans in these new areas were almost wholly eliminated by deportations combined with large scale quasi-voluntary emigration. (Thousands of Germans fled before the onrush of the Red armies.) Since the Jewish population of Poland (some three and a half million people) had been overwhelmingly exterminated in Nazi gas chambers, one of the basic and most difficult problems of pre-1939 Poland—the minority question—had virtually ceased to exist. As of 1939 less than 70 percent of the Polish population was officially reported as Roman Catholic and less than 70 percent professed to use the Polish language at home. After the war, a 95 percent homogeneity had been achieved in both respects.

But Poland's geographic shift, although it increased her economic potential and served to eliminate ethnic conflicts, was not without its negative aspects. The cession of such old historic and cultural Polish centers in the east like Lwów and Wilno to the Russians has always been a source of profound and bitter resentment among Poles generally, not just simply among the eastern emigres. It was widely regarded in the 1940s, and to some extent undoubtedly even since, as a brutal annexation forced upon Poland by a stronger and rapacious Russian neighbor. On the other hand, the occupation of the lands east of the so-called Oder-Neisse line never really received more than a qualified diplomatic consent of the Western Powers and, in turn, has always been regarded as a forced outrage by a substantial segment of German public opinion, particularly in Western Germany.[2]

Poland's losses in life and property during World War II were relatively the heaviest of all the participants in that conflict. Over 6,000,000 deaths attributed to war causes and mass extermination occurred in Poland between 1939 and 1945. Nearly 20 percent of the prewar population was destroyed during these years, a substantial majority of the victims being the Jews. As of 1949 Poland's population was still only 24.2 million as compared with an estimated 35 million in 1939. Yet, thanks to one of Europe's highest birth rates and a greatly reduced death rate since 1945, the population figure again reached the 32 million mark in mid-1960s.

The Polish people in the second half of the twentieth century, under Communist rule, not only inhabit a largely different country; they are in various ways a different nation: more urbanized, more ethnically and socially homogeneous, more industrialized, and even more generally literate than pre-war Poles. But, if war and a quarter century of Communist rule have produced startling changes in the physiognomy of modern Poland, there have also been some important continuities and links with the past. These are no less important to an adequate understanding of the dynamics of Polish political life today.

In Poland, national identity and Catholicism find common roots in a historical heritage which reaches one thousand years into the country's past.[3] In A.D. 966 the first Polish ruler, Mieszko, of the Piast dynasty, at once unified the scattered Polish tribes and converted them to Catholicism. By the beginning of the seventeenth century, Poland had established a vast empire stretching from the Black to the Baltic Sea, from the vicinity of Berlin to within a hundred miles of Moscow. Internally, the foundations for this remarkable expansion were laid in the prosperous reign of King Casimir the Great (1333–70) and subsequently in Poland's 1386 union with Lithuania, achieved through the marriage of the Polish Queen Jadwiga to the Lithuanian, and then Polish, King Władysław Jagiełło. The dynastic union brought Lithuania into the fold of the Roman Catholic Church, and was converted into a permanent or state union of Poland and Lithuania in 1569 at Lublin.

From the very beginning of her existence, Poland found herself in conflict with various eastern and Asiatic foes of Christendom, and over a period of several centuries she developed an important cultural self-identification as defender of Latin, Western, and Christian civilization against the "barbarism of the East." The Poles fought and resisted innumerable Mongol, Tartar, Cossack, and Turkish inroads on the eastern fringes of the European continent.

Probably the most famous Polish victory against eastern incursions into Europe came in 1683, when King Jan Sobieski's forces helped to save Vienna from a Turkish siege. The imperial ambitions of the Ottoman Empire in Europe were thereby dealt a decisive defeat.

Among Poland's major Christian opponents in the centuries of her expansion and decline were the German Teutonic Knights of East Prussia, the Swedes, and the rising Muscovite empire. Ultimately, it was the dynamic expansion of German Prussia under Frederick the

Great and of Russia under Peter and Catherine in the eighteenth century which brought about the final division and demise of the Polish state in successive partitions of 1772, 1793, and 1795. Long years of internal weakening, even anarchy, institutionally embodied in the famous legislative "liberum veto,"* and an almost total emasculation of royal power by a rapacious nobility prepared the way for Poland's fall. Ironically, Polish intervention against the Turks helped to save the life of the Austrian monarchy, which within a century repaid Poland's "good deed" by joining Prussia and Russia in the total destruction of Poland.

We may note, too, that in the four centuries between the reign of Casimir the Great and the decline of the Polish monarchy in the 1600s, Poland was a multi-ethnic and multi-religious commonwealth. While Catholicism was always predominant, a remarkable degree of toleration and freedom existed for all sorts of religious and ethnic groups. Germans, Jews, Armenians, Russians, Ukrainians, Lithuanians, Czechs, and Poles "coexisted" in relative harmony and peace over long periods within the frontiers of a huge Polish state. At the beginning of the eighteenth century, among European powers, only Russia and Sweden exceeded Poland's 280,000 square miles.[4] To be sure, the tradition of Polish kings successfully ruling such a heterogeneous state owed much to the as yet undeveloped national consciousness of most of the constituent populations. It also owed something to the benevolent, if selfish, indifference of Poland's large gentry class, which preferred to deal with German, Jewish, or Czech merchants and money lenders rather than sanction the development of a potentially more "troublesome" native middle class. Nevertheless, this substantial legacy of multi-ethnic statehood has exercised a profound influence on the ideologies of modern Poland. It supported contradictory but pervasive aspirations to a revival of a great power role for Poland in east-central Europe, through conciliation and moral leadership, and sometimes through domination and force.[5]

In the full perspective of her history, it is undoubtedly the Germans and the Russians who have been Poland's principal national enemies. Conflicts with various German princes and with the Holy Roman Emperors marked the very beginnings of Polish national existence under Mieszko and continued for centuries afterwards. These conflicts became particularly acute after the 1228 settlement of the Teutonic

---

*In the seventeenth century any nobleman-representative to the Polish Diet (Sejm) could, by his single dissenting voice, defeat not merely the enactment of a specific measure but nullify the whole work of the particular session of the Diet.

Order in East Prussia. The Knights' eastward incursions culminated in the wars of 1326–1343, as a consequence of which Poland was deprived of the access to the Baltic which she had gained in earlier centuries. Under Władysław Jagiełło the Poles scored one of their greatest national victories in 1410 at the Battle of Grunwald (Tannenberg). A joint Polish-Lithuanian army defeated the Teutonic Knights and avenged the previous defeats at their hands. This was, however, by no means a final victory. Conflicts resumed and resulted in the war of 1454–1466, which ended in yet another Polish success. Thereafter, until the catastrophic partition period in the eighteenth century, Polish-German wars had at last subsided. On the other hand, wars against Russia became both more frequent and significant.

The first Russo-Polish clashes occurred at least as early as the eleventh century when a Polish prince vied for the crown of Kiev. From the beginning of the sixteenth century Russo-Polish wars rapidly multiplied. The Russians struggled with Poles in the Dnieper region in 1503, and in areas adjacent to and including Smolensk in the wars of 1512–1522 and 1534–1536. Poles and Russians again fought for control of the eastern borderlands from 1557 to 1571 and from 1579 to 1582. Between 1609 and 1618, attempts by Polish princes to gain the Russian throne led to numerous armed conflicts. More wars followed from 1632 until 1634 when Poland's King, Wladyslaw IV, renounced his claims to the Russian throne; sporadic clashes with Russia, however, did not end until 1667, and they resumed again in the war of the Polish Succession, 1733–1735.

In the latter part of the eighteenth century, Russian and Prussian influence in the declining Polish commonwealth was not only widely felt but was frequently and openly supported by armed violence against the Poles. Concommitantly, Poland's numerous (between 8 and 10 percent of the population) and often poor nobility was so singularly concerned with the maintenance of its own privileges that orderly and effective government gradually became impossible. The development of trade and of towns and of the economics of national power was retarded by the near-anarchy of the nobles' rule. Illustratively, the Diet (Sejm), which met every two years, was dissolved by vetoes twelve times between 1695 and 1762 even before it could decide on the choice of a presiding officer.[6]

The King became a puppet in the hands of the quarrelsome nobility, and all other elements in the population were excluded from sharing power. Thus, Poland developed a tradition of destructive political individualism inducing, in turn, understandable attitudes of alienation, distrust of authority, frustration, and impotence among the masses of the people.[7] Many Polish nobles acted as agents of foreign powers, heedlessly accepting subsidies and bribes from them. Not until the period of the French Revolution and the emergence of an inspiring patriotic leadership of men like Tadeusz Kościuszko and Kazimierz Pułaski did widespread revulsion against such practices take root among the nobility. Despite an upsurge of patriotic and reformist activity in the 1790s, the fatal combination of internal decay, foreign pressure, and intrigue led to the three partitions which, by 1795, had altogether extinguished the Polish state.

Poland entered the nineteenth century as her dark age of national subjugation to foreign rule. Austria's Catholic monarchy apart (because it was undoubtedly Poland's least dangerous and cruel enemy), the Poles' sense of national identity was strengthened and maintained by the significant religious-cultural gulf which had always separated them from their enemies: the predominantly Orthodox Russians and, ever since the Reformation, from the Protestant Prussians as well.

In Bismarckian Germany the struggle against Catholicism and against the Poles was frequently synonymous. The Russians by their blanket persecution of Polish culture also helped to draw the link between religious and political identification ever closer. The martyrs of the Church became the martyrs of the nation. It was by no means accidental, therefore, that Catholicism became an important element in the subsequent genesis of modern Polish nationalism. On the whole, Polish patriotism and national self-identification were stimulated and magnified by the sufferings and deprivations of foreign rule which, for all practical purposes, lasted from the end of the eighteenth century until Poland's revival as an independent state in 1918. Divided among three alien empires, the Polish people underwent a far-reaching process of social, economic, and cultural change in the nineteenth century. The peasantry became economically and socially emancipated from the remnants of tutelage and feudalism. A native middle class began to emerge and challenge the polyglot German and Jewish elements for economic, social, and political mastery of the towns. Industrialization was beginning to make rapid strides in the last half of the century and aided both the emancipation of the peasant and the growth of the middle class while the nobility—Poland's famous and once omnipotent "szlachta"—continued its drastic decline. A sizeable industrial proletariat was developing in all three sections. Polish awareness, and a spirit of nationalism, were now beginning to pervade those large strata of the population which hitherto had been largely apolitical. Poland was no longer a mere preserve of the nobility. Powerful pressures for democracy, constitutionalism, independence, and even socialism were beginning to grow at the grass roots of popular politics. The new tendencies were already in evidence, embryonically at least, in the time of Kościuszko's 1794 rising against Poland's chief aggressor—Russia—and implicit in the abortive constitution of May 3, 1791. Two other major risings took place in 1830 and 1863. Both of these were directed against the principal occupant of Polish soil—Russia. Both ended in failure and in both cases harsh repressions were meted out to the rebellious Poles. Thousands of people were imprisoned, executed, and exiled to the wastes of Siberia. But the spirit of Polish nationalism was hardly extinguished. It was rather enriched and gradually extended among all of the Polish people. The cry of Poland's great romantic poet, Adam Mickiewicz: "Fatherland, you are like health, only he who has lost you can appreciate you," became the theme of whole generations born under foreign rule and dedicated to the reestablishment of Polish independence.

Yet, on the whole, the Poland of the nineteenth century was still backward socially and economically. The great majority of the population consisted of an illiterate peasantry with minimal awareness of, and interest in, politics. A really active political life was still predominantly the province of a small but growing intelligentsia recruited from the upper and middle classes. To some extent the tendency to apathy and stagnation, implicit in the low level of mass culture in Poland, was reinforced by the failure of the last great rising of 1863. The disaster of that insurrection made the idea of a permanent accommodation with foreign rule seem unavoidable and even attractive to some Poles. The outlook for unification and independence seemed distant at best. But outright "capitulationism" proved short-lived.

A major consequence of the setback was the development of the so-called "organic work" orientation among Poles of the post '63 period. This orientation finds some interesting current parallels in Poland. The proponents of "organic work" struggled for the maintenance of Polish culture, language, traditions, schools, and institutions, without hopelessly challenging, or openly provoking, the preponderant strength of foreign rule. They tried to develop a "survival strategy" which found wide appeal in the ranks of Poland's growing intelligentsia. By the turn of the century, Polish public opinion was clearly swinging behind overtly patriotic and nationalist movements. The first and numerically most important of these was the Polish League founded in 1887. It subsequently became in 1897 the National Democratic Party of Poland. Under the leadership of Jan Ludwik Popławski, Zygmunt Balicki and, above all, Roman Dmowski (1864–1939), it soon established itself as a predominant force in Polish politics, particularly among the emergent middle class. Dmowski hoped to rebuild Poland as a unified national entity with Russian help and protection and to make her a bulwark against Germany's traditional "Drang-nach-osten." In Dmowski's view, the long range interests of Poles and Russians coincided against the great danger of German expansionism.

Numerically much smaller but ultimately a highly significant political grouping was the Polish Socialist Party founded in 1893. One of its early leaders was Józef Piłsudski who became Poland's Chief of State in 1918.

Piłsudski differed with Dmowski, above all, in the assessment of Poland's principal enemy and in the means required for restoring Polish independence. He hoped and worked for yet another armed insurrection against Russia at an opportune moment. Where Piłsudski articulated the resentments of those Poles who were bitter at the barbaric cruelty of the Tsar's rule in Poland, Dmowski believed that only Germany's—not Russia's—national interest precluded acquiescence in the eventual revival and maintenance of a Polish state. Dmowski believed that Russia would ultimately realize her own interest in the reestablishment of a strong Polish state. She was Poland's natural ally, he argued, and the task of statesmanship was to persuade her of this, not to attack her. Hence, Dmowski regarded both the objective of the insurrection and the method as a folly and even a reckless crime against the interest of the Polish nation.[8]

Yet, the Polish state which emerged out of World War I owed a great deal to both leaders and movements. During the first World War, Piłsudski led armed Polish Legions against the Russians on the side of Germany and Austria. Dmowski supported Russia, Britain, France, and ultimately the United States against Germany and Austria. When the resistance of the central powers collapsed, Pilsudski's legionnaires furnished the nucleus of a Polish army inside Poland and Piłsudski himself the nucleus of public authority when German forces retreated from Poland in the wake of the 1918 Armistice. Dmowski, in the natural and plausible guise of the West's ally, represented Poland at the Versailles Conference and fought with considerable success for Poland's new frontiers. In this task he was greatly aided by the commitment of President Wilson to the restoration of an independent Poland and to the principle of the self-determination of nations.

The existence of the revived Polish state of 1919 was almost immediately jeopardized by the invasion of the Soviet army into Poland in 1920, following Piłsudski's own expedition into the Ukraine. A catastrophe was barely averted at the gates of Warsaw. In this conflict, the minuscule Communist party of Poland, siding with the Russian invaders in the name of "proletarian internationalism," went a long way towards becoming discredited as a political force of any consequence among the Polish people.

The period between 1919 and 1939 saw a necessarily difficult attempt on the part of the Poles to rebuild a state which was no more than a cherished memory of a distant past. Three sections of the country, each for over a century under a different foreign power, had to be welded together into a coherent unity. Polish experience in self-government was at once scant and diverse. If the deprivations of foreign rule contributed something to a heightened sense of national identification and patriotism among Poles, they were not without negative influence on civic attitudes. People learned to look upon political authority as alien, hostile, and imposed from without. The government, the tax collector, the policeman, and the public works inspector were seen across a deep gulf of "we" versus "they." This peculiar experience with government was undoubtedly a factor in shaping Polish individualism and civic attitudes: away from cooperation with, and trust in, political organs and toward a more escapist, and even anarchist "devil may care" type of outlook.[9]

Internal reconstruction and development were also complicated by the fundamental dilemma of reconciling a very substantial, integral Polish nationalism with the successful operation of a multi-ethnic state and with the counter claims of non-Polish nationalisms. All of the minority groups demanded state recognition and support for their cultural, religious, and linquistic identity. Some Jewish groups demanded various forms of autonomous self-government on the local level. Ukrainian and Byelorussian groups pressed in some cases for ultimate independence from Poland, and in most for territorial autonomy within the Polish state. All minorities insisted on the rights of equal citizenship with Poles in the new state.

The large and influential body of Polish opinion, however, whose spokesman was Roman Dmowski, stood firmly committed to a program of integral Polish nationalism. It envisioned a state based on the undisputed primacy of the Polish nation and was unwilling to genuinely accommodate these minority claims. Thus, national conflict was one of the main themes of Polish politics in the years between 1918 and 1939, and, given the size of the minority groups, it was a major stumbling block to genuine stability in the Polish State.[10]

(It may be observed, parenthetically, that the remarkable current revival of an official anti-Semitism in People's Poland—particularly by the Moczar faction of the Communist Party—is rooted in an intense

anti-Semitism long advocated by Dmowski and his Nationalist followers.)[11]

Politically, the interwar period may be divided into two phases.
From 1919 to 1926 Poland maintained a parliamentary regime patterned on the model of the French III Republic. In May 1926, Marshal
Józef Piłsudski, erstwhile Chief of State, overthrew the parliamentary
Wojciechowski-Witos regime and gradually established a dictatorship
based, to a great extent, on his original World War I Legionnaire
following but with significant support from the army, bureaucracy,
landed interests, and clergy among the elites of Polish society. In
addition, Piłsudski personally commanded a significant popular following among the broad masses of the Polish people, among peasants,
workers, and initially even among minority nationalities.[12] A leader of
many personal and intellectual gifts, Piłsudski was a charismatic personality, something of a legendary hero in Poland's struggle for independence long before he seized power in 1926. Before World War I
he had been instrumental in identifying a majority of the Polish socialist movement with both national patriotism and democracy. He came
to power widely regarded as a "Man of the Left," the erstwhile socialist
conspirator against Tsardom, but also remembered as a patriot and
victorious leader of the Polish armies in 1921.

The overt purposes of Piłsudski's *coup* were to put an end to the
division and factional strife which plagued Poland's politics under its
multi-party parliamentary regime. He promised to fight against
"prywata"* and to bring strong and decisive government on behalf of
the public weal. Piłsudski's rule was autocratic but hardly totalitarian
in a Nazi or Stalinist sense. Opposition parties and press were allowed
to operate, subject to intermittent rather than massive or continuous
harassments. Power shifted from Parliament, where opposition was
allowed both representation and expression, to the Cabinet, where
decisions were subject to Piłsudski's wishes.

Piłsudski shied away from undertaking any substantial social and
economic reforms and devoted his main energies to strengthening the
Polish state primarily in a political-administrative and military sense.
His years in power coincided with the catastrophic impact on Poland
of the world depression in the 1929–1935 period. He and his regime
gradually became alienated from the bulk of the Left and the ethnic
minorities, while winning considerable backing among the traditionally conservative and right-wing strata of Polish society. Following the
1928 elections in which Piłsudski's so-called nonpartisan organization,

---

*selfish, personal interests.

the B.B.W.R., (Bezpartyjny Blok Współpracy z Rządem or Nonpartisan Bloc of Cooperation with the Government) failed to win a majority, Piłsudski's regime became increasingly repressive. In 1930 numerous leaders of Polish opposition parties were arrested, jailed and mal- treated as a prelude to the national elections. A harsh "pacification campaign" was carried out against the Ukrainian population of Po- land's eastern and southeastern provinces. When the Marshal's sup- porters, the B.B.W.R., at last obtained an obviously tarnished majority in the 1930 election, they devoted themselves to far reaching constitu- tional reform. In 1935 a new constitution was adopted which tilted the formal structure of government in Poland heavily in favor of executive (Presidential) power, and diminished the role of the legislature which had been, theoretically, at least, preponderant under the previous Polish Constitution of 1921. In the same year, however, Piłsudski died, and his followers were left without their essential asset—the legendary personality who legitimized their power in the eyes of millions of Poles, and one whose unquestioned fiat imposed outward unity among his followers. After Piłsudski's death the regime continued under a far less popular coterie of his heirs (often referred to as "colonels"). Notable among this ruling group were President Mościcki, Marshal Rydz Śmigły, the Foreign Minister Colonel Józef Beck, and Premier General Felicjan Sławoj-Składkowski.

In the ensuing period, from 1935 to 1939, the government became more and more isolated from public opinion and internally divided. After the implementation of the electoral law of 1935 all opposition parties were effectively excluded even from token parliamentary repre- sentation.

In 1936 the B.B.W.R. gave way to a new political organization of the ruling group. It became the O.Z.N. (Obóz Zjednoczenia Narodowego or Camp of National Unity). The new organization at once expressed and strengthened the tendency toward neo-fascist, ultra-nationalist, and totalitarian orientations within the regime. Mounting interna- tional crises, lack of widespread popular following for, and disunity among Piłsudski's heirs (some of whom, like President Mościcki, doubted the virtues of a Nazi-like dictatorship) rendered the political prospects in 1938–1939 uncertain. Some observers expected the regime to give in to grass roots pressures for "liberalization"; others expected, or feared, increasingly repressive measures.

Poland on the eve of the War in 1939 was still a largely agricultural, economically backward, and relatively underdeveloped nation. The Polish peasant was most frequently either an economically marginal small-holder or landless. The underdevelopment of Polish industry, which lacked investment funds for expansion, made it impossible to relieve the chronic unemployment and underemployment in the Polish countryside. The progress of land reform, on which the peasants set high hopes, was far too slow and marginal to satisfy their demands. In the last few years of the regime there were widespread peasant strikes and demonstrations. Illiteracy, malnutrition and related diseases, like tuberculosis, were all serious problems both in rural and urban areas. Industrial unemployment was both widespread and severe throughout the 1930s. The tensions and conflicts between Polish nationalists, within and without the O.Z.N., and the ethnic minorities, particularly Ukrainian and Jewish, grew sharper and more difficult daily.

The regime of Piłsudski's heirs confronted the threat of imminent war with scant material resources and without the presence and prestige of their great leader. It was not until Hitler's actual attack on Poland on September 1, 1939, that the government found itself supported by a genuine consensus of Polish patriotic opinion. Internal differences were forgotten and the country stood united in the face of Nazi invasion. But, with allied Britain and France giving Poland virtually no aid, direct or indirect, Polish troops reeled before the onslaught of the vastly stronger, mechanized German *Wehrmacht* and *Luftwaffe*.

On September 17 Russia's Red Army invaded Poland from the east. Twenty years of Polish independence had come to an end.[13] In what became the fourth partition of Poland pursuant to the Molotov-Ribbentrop pact, Nazi Germany and the Soviet Union divided up the whole territory of the Polish State. For the world at large the most cataclysmic conflict yet had just begun.[14] For the Poles, September 1939 was also the latest version of a basic theme of their history: destruction at the hands of two traditional great enemies. All that remained of the Polish State after September 1939 was a Government-in-Exile, first in Paris then in London, and a substantial number of Polish soldiers, sailors, and airmen who continued the struggle against the Nazis on foreign soil. For many of these Poles exile became permanent as Poland passed directly from Nazi occupation to Communist rule in the course of the war.

The Communist seizure of power, as elsewhere in Eastern Europe, was a multistage process. It was not essentially completed in Poland until the end of 1948. In pursuit of power the Communists enjoyed one obvious advantage—the military and diplomatic backing of the Soviet Union—and one equally obvious disadvantage—the lack of substantial popular support among the Polish people.

Prewar Communism in Poland had never put down deep roots. Its internationalism, atheism, and after 1917, patent identification with

Russia made it thoroughly unpalatable to the vast majority of Poles. In the election of 1928 the Communist Party (KPP) reached the high water mark of its popularity among the Polish electorate, polling about 8 percent of the national vote. Even this modest result must be substantially discounted by the disproportionate following which the Communists enjoyed among Poland's politically alienated ethnic minority groups.[15] The Party operated, in fact, as an illegal organization during most of the 1919–1939 period, and the Piłsudski regime, particularly, subjected it to stringent police controls and criminal prosecution. The Party was plagued by grave internal dissension between the Trotskyite and Stalinist wings in the late 1920s and 1930s, and finally, in 1938, it was dissolved altogether by Stalin on the grounds that it had been "infiltrated by enemy agents."[16] With its principal leaders "liquidated," no national communist organization, not even a quasi-communist one, operated in Poland until 1942.

Indeed, from September 1939 until June 1941, when Germany tore up the Ribbentrop-Molotov pact by attacking Russia, no political party ideologically affiliated with the USSR would have been able to address any plausible appeals to the Polish people. Stalin treated the Polish territories annexed in 1939 as integral parts of the USSR and carried out mass deportations of the local Polish population into remote, Asiatic regions of the Soviet Union. According to some estimates, no fewer than one and a half million persons were deported by the Russians to forced labor camps in the Soviet Union.[17] Thousands of these people simply perished from cold and hunger. In 1940, unknown as yet to most of the world, the Soviets executed some 4,000 captured Polish officers in Russia's Katyn forest.[18] During the whole period of the Hitler-Stalin alliance, the USSR stood utterly indifferent and wholly passive in the face of the even more numerous crimes and brutalities committed by the Nazis in the western part of Poland. In those days, officially, at least, Poland was simply a Marxian "unproblem"!

Hitler's implementation of the plan "Barbarossa" drastically changed the political situation. Stalin was eager to get whatever help he could from Britain and the United States in his mortal confrontation with Nazism. The Western powers saw undeniable advantage in enlisting Soviet support in the struggle against Hitler. For the Polish Government in London, then, Russia had suddenly become an "allies' ally" and potentially even a future liberator.

Diplomatic relations between the USSR and the London Poles were established in August 1941. General Sikorski, the Prime Minister of the Polish Government-in-Exile, went to Moscow in December 1941 to help implement a "Declaration of Amnesty" by which the Soviet government promised to release all Polish citizens held prisoner in the USSR. He also hoped to organize, from among these, a Polish army that would fight side by side with the Russians against the Nazis under the command of General Władysław Anders, heretofore held as a prisoner of war by the Russians.

In January 1942 the hitherto defunct Polish Communist Party was revived under the more innocuous name of Polish Workers' Party (PPR). Among its founders were Bolesław Bierut and Władysław Gomułka. Much of the new party's personnel was actually parachuted and infiltrated into German-occupied Poland from the USSR. Its immediate tasks, as defined by the Party itself, were to construct a broad, "patriotic" front of opposition to and sabotage of the German war effort in Poland. This limited objective was followed within a year (March 1, 1943) by the enunciation of the Party's goals for a postwar Polish state. All of these goals were still sufficiently generalized and innocuous to enable the Communists to bid for maximum support from various non-Communist elements towards the realization of common objectives. They called for a liquidation of prewar reactionary rule; a thoroughgoing land reform; substantial nationalization of major industries and a foreign policy based on friendship with the USSR. There was no enunciation of Marxism-Leninism, the dictatorship of the proletariat, collectivization, suppression of opposition, or similar overtly Communist themes. The Party geared itself to the tactics of a united front. In May of 1942, the PPR created its own underground army, the so-called *Gwardia Ludowa* or G.L. (People's Guard) subsequently renamed *Armia Ludowa* or A.L. (People's Army). This relatively small resistance unit was opposed by the Communists (PPR) to the older and far larger Polish underground movement, the *Armia Krajowa* or A.K. (Home Army). The latter was an arm of the London-based Polish Government-in-Exile. The Communists attempted to discredit it by charging it with a do-nothing attitude toward the Nazi enemy and hostility toward the Soviet Union. Where the Home Army was anxious to minimize German executions and repressions against Polish civilians for guerrilla acts of sabotage, the Communists did not have such scruples. They attempted to capitalize on the population's hatred of the Nazi rulers without worrying unduly about consequences, and they thus adopted the pose of maximum underground activisim.

In early 1943 the Germans disclosed the discovery of mass graves of Polish officers at Katyn, attributing the crime to the Russians. When the Polish Government in London expressed concern and asked for an investigation by the International Red Cross in Geneva, the Soviets used this as a pretext for severing diplomatic relations with the London Poles in April of 1943.

The Soviet press announced in April the creation of a "Union of Polish Patriots" in the USSR, led by the Polish writer Wanda Wasilewska (wife of A. Korneychuk, subsequently Deputy Foreign Minister of the Soviet Union) and a number of obscure prewar communists, including Stefan Jędrychowski, Aleksander Zawadzki, Stanisław Radkiewicz, and Hilary Minc.

This group was the nucleus of an alternative, Communist-led government that the Soviets were preparing for a subsequent take-over of Poland, even while they maintained normal diplomatic relations with the London Poles. At about the same time, the Soviets began to form a Polish division under the command of a prewar Polish lieutenant-colonel, Zygmunt Berling. This division, named after Kościuszko, was provided with a substantial Polish Communist and Soviet leadership. It was the nucleus of the future army of People's Poland and was assembled primarily from among Russian-held Polish POWs.*

Within a few months, new, rival forms of underground Polish political authority were created under Soviet and Communist auspices. The first of these was a provisional parliament called Krajowa Rada Narodowa or KRN (National Council of the Homeland) said to have been organized in a clandestine meeting in Warsaw in December 1943. This new group claimed to be a multiparty body representative of broad strata of Polish public opinion. Actually, it was overwhelmingly dominated by the Communists, although it included a few others, like the subsequent Premier and left-wing Socialist, Edward Osóbka-Morawski. The creation of the KRN, publicized by Moscow, was the first open indication that the USSR would sponsor a full-fledged claimant to power in Poland as a rival to the London group, hitherto recognized by all the allies as the legitimate government of Poland. Further implementation of this objective of "rival authority" was the creation on Soviet-occupied Polish territory (at Chełm) on July 21, 1944 of a Polish Committee of National Liberation (PKWN or *Polski Komitet Wyzwolenia Narodowego*) which was no less than the executive body or a provisional "cabinet" of the quasi-parliamentary KRN. Osóbka-Morawski became its chairman or "Premier," although again all the key posts were Communist-controlled. On July 22, 1944 the PKWN issued a manifesto to the Polish people in which it claimed to be the

---

*About 75,000 Polish soldiers and officers, led by General Anders, were allowed to leave for the Middle East during 1942. They subsequently fought side by side with British and U.S. troops in North Africa and Italy.

sole legal source of political authority in the country and which set out
the group's program for the future. The manifesto's planks were all in
keeping with the moderate and "patriotic" line set by PPR in 1943.
Land reform; expansion of western frontiers at Germany's expense;
democratization of Polish life; friendship with the USSR—these were
among its relatively consensual themes. On December 31, 1944 the
PKWN unilaterally proclaimed itself the Provisional Government of
Poland (with temporary headquarters in Lublin) and was recognized
as such by the USSR on January 5, 1945.

As the Soviet armies advanced westward against the retreating Nazis, members of the London-affiliated (AK) resistance movement
whom they encountered were being rounded up, arrested, and even
occasionally executed. The most important "liquidation" of non-Communist resistance in Poland however, occurred at German hands in
Warsaw during August and September of 1944. On August 1 the
Polish London-affiliated underground began an insurrection in the
capital and fought the Nazis in the streets, seeking to liberate Warsaw
in advance of the approaching Red Army. While the Red forces paused
and, in the main, passively watched, the Polish underground fighters
and the capital's nearly one and a half million people were subjected
to a cataclysmic liquidation.[19] Several hundred thousand persons were
killed, or severly wounded; many were subsequently deported to concentration camps at Oświecim (Auschwitz) and elsewhere; the city was
reduced to ruins. Warsaw's Polish commander, General Bór-
Komorowski, went to a German POW camp and the city was liberated
next year, in 1945, not by London-affiliated Poles but by Russians—
a wholly depopulated pile of rubble.

Simultaneously with Moscow's resurrection and reorganization of
Polish Communism in Russia and in Poland, the Soviet government
pressed on with intense diplomatic activity pointed toward the same
basic objective: the absorption of Poland into the Soviet political domain. At no time after the outbreak of Nazi-Soviet hostilities in June
1941 did Stalin relent from the view that the territories the USSR
annexed from Poland in 1939 were in fact rightfully Soviet. These
areas accounted for 47 percent of prewar Poland and Stalin's continued claim to them was, from 1941 onwards, the major single source
of conflict in the relations between Moscow and the London Poles.
The historic turning point in the fate of the Polish Government-in-
exile came in March of 1943 when, unbeknown to them and in apparent contradiction to the principles of the 1941 Atlantic Charter, President Roosevelt and Prime Minister Churchill agreed "in principle" to
the cession, by Poland, of her eastern regions to the USSR, with some

Poland's Frontiers, 1939 and 1945

territorial compensations to be provided for at the expense of Germany in the west. Stalin, having succeeded in convincing Britain and the United States of the validity and basic irrefutability of his claims, succeeded also in the diplomatic isolation and the weakening of the London Poles at the same time. In an October 1944 Moscow conference, Winston Churchill himself pressured the then Polish Premier-in-exile, Stanisław Mikołajczyk, to accept Stalin's territorial claims.[20] By the end of 1944, Polish opposition to these claims was viewed as senseless intransigence even by the Western powers. Significantly, Churchill sought to persuade Mikołajczyk on the grounds that territorial concessions to Russia would make Stalin give up his attempt to rule Poland through an all-Communist government.[21] But in 1944 Soviet diplomacy was no longer content with territorial claims against the Poles. It demanded the lion's share of influence in the future government of the country. This aspiration was soon realized.

The Yalta conference in February 1945 served not only to affirm Soviet territorial claims on Poland but also resulted in an Allied agreement to establish a "Provisional Government of National Unity" in the country: in effect a coalition between Communists and non-Communists, albeit with assurances to the Western Powers that free elections would ultimately be held. In June 1945 such a Government was at last established. Out of the twenty-one cabinet posts included, fourteen went to the Communist-led Lublin group. Within a few days, two more Communist ministers were added, so that the anti-Communists and the non-Communists, headed by the former London Prime Minister (now Vice-Premier and Minister of Agriculture) Mikołajczyk, were, from the outset, hopelessly outnumbered. On July 5, 1945 the governments of the United States and Great Britain extended diplomatic recognition to this new Polish regime while simultaneously withdrawing their recognition of the London exiles. Thus, the new regime had acquired a significant cloak of legitimacy in operations in and outside Poland. It became the internationally recognized government of Poland.

The only legal and effectively organized political opposition to the Communists in Poland in 1945 was the PSL (Peasant Party or *Polskie Stronnictwo Ludowe*) led by Mikołajczyk. The Communists simply prevented various other potential opposition parties, in particular the prewar Nationalists, from legally organizing. The charges of fascism, subversion and, above all, collaboration with the Nazis were levelled against these groups. The Communist PPR attempted to broaden its support by the creation of a so-called Democratic Bloc in alliance with three other groups. The first of these was the Polish Socialist Party,

(PPS or *Polska Partia Socjalistyczna*) which, with Communist and Soviet help, was placed under the control of a pro-Communist leadership under Józef Cyrankiewicz and Edward Osóbka-Morawski. Two ephemeral and largely artificial groups were represented in the Bloc by the so-called Populist Party (SL or *Stronnictwo Ludowe*) and the Democratic Party (SD or *Stronnictwo Demokratyczne*). While the PPS had been a well established political force in Poland since before 1939, the latter two parties were in effect newly created Communist front organizations. Mikołajczyk's position as the leader of the only legal opposition in Poland made him at once the hope of all the anti-Communists and the target of Communist terror and intimidation. The national election staged in January 1947, prepared by strong-arm tactics and characterized by mass falsification of the results, gave the Communist PPR and its allies all but twenty-seven of the 444 seats in a single chamber constituent assembly *(Sejm)*. Western protests before and after the election proved wholly unavailing.²² Mikołajczyk was ousted from the cabinet and his PSL was subjected to systematic persecution by the Polish Security Police (UB or *Urząd Bezpieczeństwa* often referred to by the Poles as *"Bezpieka"*). This organization was in fact a conglomerate of Soviet security police agents and selected Polish-Communist recruits.

Indeed, throughout the formative years of the Communist regime, from 1944 to 1948, Soviet armed forces acted as a reserve lever and auxiliary of the regime. The arrests and deportations to the USSR of the anti-Communist Polish underground leaders, like General Niedzwiadek Okulicki and Jankowski in March 1945, were amply illustrative. In several parts of Poland sporadic guerrilla warfare was being waged against the new regime by remnants of the anti-Communist underground groups. At the end of 1947 Mikołajczyk himself fled to the west and his party dissolved amidst Communist charges of espionage and treason.

The last major "undigested element" on the Polish political scene passed under Communist control when the PPR forced a merger with the numerically stronger and—so far as rank and file opinion was concerned—reluctant PPS, into a single Polish United Workers' Party (PZPR or *Polska Zjednoczona Partia Robotnicza*) in December 1948. In the same year, in September, the balance within the ruling Communist PPR had tilted dramatically in favor of the Muscovite and obediently pro-Soviet segment of the party, with the expulsion of Gomułka and his "nationalist deviationist" associates from the Party's Central Committee. The initial phase of "Communization" and "Stalinization" was thus completed.²³

The legacy of the Second World War and the relationship between Soviet Russia and Polish Communism are problems which have continuing significance for Poland today. They are not "mere" history. The Communist regime, under Gomułka and before him, has attempted to win popular support by espousing its own interpretations of the pre-1945 developments. The Communists have tried to dispel the widespread notions that (a) Soviet Russian policies have been hostile to Poland and that (b) their own party was essentially an agency of this hostile foreign power. Obviously as long as the bulk of the Polish people should see Polish Communism in such terms, the party's rule could not be accepted as legitimate. Hence party propaganda in Poland had developed its own version of national betrayal which it attributes to the prewar regime, to the London exiles, and to all political parties and leaders supporting the one and the other. In this view, prewar Poland is seen as not really independent but actually a pawn of foreign capitalist interests. Piłsudski's government is described as fascist and harboring imperialist designs on the USSR. Above all, the Communists see the prewar regime as responsible for Poland's defeat in 1939 because of what they regard as deliberately anti-Soviet and pro-Nazi policies pursued by Colonel Beck in the 1930s. The Communists view the German attack on Poland as having been inevitable and unbeatable without Soviet help, which the Polish leadership is said to have shunned and rejected. Britain and France in the late 1930s are pictured as more interested in turning Nazi aggression against Communist Russia than in helping the Poles. The Polish prewar leadership is presented as seeking primarily to maintain its power in Poland, even at the expense of national independence, and of "criminal connivance against the USSR." Soviet annexation of eastern Poland is pictured as preventing the extension of Nazi power eastward and as an act of liberation and protection of Ukrainians and Byelorussians.

As for the occupation period, from 1939 to 1944, the Communists see the London exiles as continuers of a policy of betrayal. Under the slogan of opposing two enemies—Germany and Russia—the exiles are said to have been more anti-Soviet than anti-German, to have been little concerned with resistance toward Nazism and much more concerned with opposing Russia and Communism. The deportations of Poles by the Russians in 1939–1941 are all but forgotten. The Katyn forest massacre is presented as merely "Goebbels' propaganda trick" and attributed to the Germans. The Warsaw uprising is seen as a "criminal and reckless provocation" by the London exiles bent on seizing power for themselves under circumstances when the Red

Army, from a military point of view, (allegedly) could not offer effective assistance to Warsaw. The Communists similarly dispute the view that they themselves emerged in 1942 as a tool of Soviet policy. According to Gomułka's recent pronouncements, the founding of the National Council of the Homeland (KRN) in 1943 came as surprise news to the Russians.[24] Gomułka had on various occasions emphasized that the PPR during the war depended to a great extent on its own resources.

Even after 1956, however, Polish Communist leadership has assiduously cultivated the image of an always helpful and benevolent Russian neighbor, whose friendship has been, is, and will be, indispensable to the maintenance of genuine independence and social progress in Poland. If the Russians have ever—since the Bolshevik Revolution— behaved "incorrectly" toward Poles, this is attributed solely to "Stalinism."

When Edward Gierek succeeded Gomułka in 1970, alliance and friendship with the USSR were among his first public pledges. The Party press has emphasized the contention that Gierek's reforms—his wage increases and price freezes—have been made possible only because of the generosity of Soviet loans and credits.

Having surveyed some of the major background themes of Poland's history, we may more readily consider the institutions and politics of the present regime.

NOTES

1. Among Polish sources see K. Symmons-Symonolewicz, "Polish Political Thought and the Problem of the Eastern Borderlands of Poland, 1918–1939, *Polish Review*, vol. IV, No. 1–2, 1959, pp. 65–81 and Stainsław Estreicher, *Dziesięciolecie Polski Odrodzonej 1918–1928* (Warsaw, 1929), pp. 215–18. See also *Rocznik Polityczny i Gospodarczy*, P. A. T. (Warsaw, 1939), pp. 14–20. Władysław Pobóg-Malinowski, *Najnowsza Historia polityczna Polski, 1864–1945*, vol. II, Paris, 1956.

2. See e.g., Z. M. Szaz, *Germany's Eastern Frontiers: The Problem of the Oder-Neisse Line* (Chicago, 1960). Also Wolfgang Wagner, *The Genesis of the Oder-Neisse Line* (Stuttgart, 1957), and Herbert Feis, *Churchill, Roosevelt, Stalin* (Princeton, 1957).

3. On Polish history see Oskar Halecki, *A History of Poland* (New York, 1943), and *Borderlands of Western Civilization: A History of East*

Central Europe (New York, 1952); Roman Dyboski, *Poland* (New York, 1933); T. Komarnicki, *Rebirth of the Polish Republic: A Study in the Diplomatic History of Europe 1914–1920* (London, 1957).

4. See Robert Ergang, *Europe From the Renaissance to Waterloo*, (Boston, 1954), p. 535.

5. See e.g., M. K. Dziewanowski's *Joseph Piłsudski: A European Federalist 1918–1922* (Stanford, 1969), and also A. J. Groth, "Dmowski, Piłsudski and Ethnic Conflict in pre-1939 Poland" *Canadian Slavic Studies*, vol. III, no. 1, Spring 1969, pp. 60–91.

6. Ergang, *op. cit.*, p. 537.

7. Cf. James F. Morrison, *The Polish People's Republic*, (Baltimore, 1968), on themes which may be regarded as inputs to Polish political culture, pp. 3–14.

8. On this theme see Adam Bromke, *Poland's Politics: Idealism vs. Realism* (Cambridge, Mass., 1967), pp. 7–51 particularly. The works of Poland's principal ideologist of nationalism, Roman Dmowski, (1864–1939) have not been translated into English; they are, however, available in the United States. *Myśli Nowoczesnego Polaka* (The Thoughts of a Modern Pole) of 1903 was particularly influential. Some interesting insights into the genesis of similarly extremist forms of nationalism as responses to political deprivation (i.e. lack of one's own unified national state) may be found, among others, in Louis L. Snyder, *The Meaning of Nationalism* (New York, 1954). See also Hans Kohn, *Nationalism: Its Meaning and History* (New York, 1955).

9. There has been no study of Polish politics comparable to G. Almond and S. Verba's *Civic Culture* (Boston, 1963). The evidence about substantial civic alienation in Poland is strongly suggested by a variety of sources ranging from prewar memoirs of Polish statesmen (Piłsudski and Witos, e.g.) to recent surveys of university students' attitudes toward politics in Poland. See *infra.*

10. On minority problems from non Polish sources see Simon Segal, *The New Poland and the Jews* (New York, 1938); also S. Horak, *Poland and Her National Minorities, 1919–1939* (New York, 1962).

11. In his 1934 book, *Przewrót*, Dmowski endorsed and praised Hitler's anti-Semitism, pp. 489–93. Reiterating his ideas going back to at least 1903, he then wrote: "Even if Jews were morally angels, mentally geniuses, even if they were people of a higher kind than we are, the very fact of their existence among us and their close participation in our life is for our society lethal and they have got to be rid of" [Trzeba się ich pozbyć] (p. 309). See also A. J. Groth, "The Legacy of Three Crises: Parliament and Ethnic Issues in Prewar Poland" *Slavic Review*, vol. XXVII, no. 4, December 1968, pp. 564–80.

12. The nature and evolution of the Piłsudski regime have been a subject of controversy. Among others see William J. Rose, *The Rise of Polish Democracy* (London 1944); S. L. Sharp, *Poland, White Eagle on a Red Field* (Cambridge, 1953). See also J. Rothschild, "The Ideological, Political and Economic Background of Piłsudski's *Coup d'Etat* of 1926," *Political Science Quarterly*, LXXVII, June, 1963, pp. 224–44. On the nature of that regime's electoral clientele see A. J. Groth, "Polish Elections 1919–1928," *Slavic Review*, vol. XXIV, no. 4, December 1965, pp. 653–65.

13. On this period see R. L. Buell, *Poland: Key to Europe* (New York, 1939), Robert Machray, *The Poland of Piłsudski* (New York, 1936), and Joseph Rothschild, *Piłsudski's Coup d'Etat* (New York, 1966).

14. On the subject of Polish interwar policy see Roman Debicki, *The Foreign Policy of Poland, 1919–1939* (New York, 1962); also Josef Korbel, *Poland Between East and West: Soviet and German Diplomacy Toward Poland 1919–1933* (Princeton, 1963).

15. See R. V. Burks, *The Dynamics of Communism in Eastern Europe* (Princeton, 1961), chapter 8 and 10. The reasons for the greater appeal of communism to groups and persons alienated from their social environment are explored by Gabriel Almond, *The Appeals of Communism* (Princeton, 1954), chs. 7–10. See also Hadley Cantril, *The Politics of Despair* (New York, 1962). Cf. Paul E. Zinner, *Revolution in Hungary* (New York, 1962), pp. 80–81 on the ingestion of Jewish intellectuals into the Party cadres in Hungary.

16. See Richard Hiscocks, *Poland, Bridge for the Abyss?* (New York, 1963), pp. 76–77. It is likely that the dissolution of the KPP was considered by Stalin a necessary prelude to his "deal" with Hitler wiping Poland off the map of Europe.

17. See particularly Edward J. Rozek, *Allied Wartime Diplomacy: A Pattern in Poland* (New York, 1958), pp. 46–7.

18. See the exhaustive account by J. K. Zawodny, *Death in the Forest: The Katyn Forest Massacre* (Notre Dame, 1962).

19. See T. Bór-Komorowski, *The Secret Army* (New York, 1951).

20. See Stanisław Mikołajczyk, *The Rape of Poland: Pattern of Soviet Aggression* (New York, 1948), pp. 66–90. Cf. Rozek *op. cit.*, pp. 235–264.

21. See e.g., J. Ciechanowski's *Defeat in Victory* (New York, 1947); Mikołajczyk *op. cit.*, pp. 91–105; Winston S. Churchill, *Triumph and Tragedy* (Boston, 1953), pp. 226 ff.; see also A. J. Groth "Churchill and Stalin's Russia," *Bucknell Review*, vol. XIV, no. 1, March 1966, pp. 74–94.

22. See Arthur Bliss Lane, *I Saw Poland Betrayed* (Indianapolis,

1948), and H. Peter Stern, *The Struggle for Poland* (Washington, D.C., 1953), pp. 45 ff.

23. For a comparison with other "take-overs" in east-central Europe see Hugh Seton-Watson, *The East European Revolution* (New York, 1961), Part III.

24. Gomułka's view is presented at length in his *Przemówienia* (speeches) (Warsaw, 1963), pp. 7–41.

2

The Institutions

Like the Soviet Union and other East European Communist nations, Poland has a dual structure of power: Party and State. The actual government of the country reflects the fusion of the two pyramids or hierarchies of power, and the apparatus of the Party is in substantial control of the apparatus of the State.

In this chapter we survey briefly some of the major institutional instruments of Party control. 1956, the year of Gomułka's return to power, is a significant date in the development of Polish political institutions. It separates Stalinist from post-Stalinist Poland. Our discussion here, as well as in subsequent chapters, focuses upon the differences between these two periods and the changes since 1956.

The present Polish constitution was adopted in July 1952, at the height of the Stalinist domination of what used to be the "Soviet Bloc" in Eastern Europe. Appropriately enough, it was patterned largely on the Soviet, so-called "Stalin Constitution" of 1936.

In its preamble, the Polish law attributes Poland's national independence to the "victory of the USSR over fascism" and pays tribute to the Soviet Union's primacy and leadership among workers and peasants' states. It is notable for its large Bill of Rights which ranges from such socio-economic guarantees as the right to work, leisure, and education, to political rights in the traditional western democratic sense, like freedom of speech, press, assembly and religious worship.[1]

This "liberalism" of the Polish Constitution is tempered, however, by provisions which prohibit the organization of groups "threatening the political and social structure" of Poland and by a long list of citizens' duties which could be readily invoked to deny rights to the enemies of the state. Unlike the Soviet Constitution the Polish charter does not specifically assign the role of leader and vanguard to the

Communist party. The Polish system is defined constitutionally as a People's Democratic State, a state entity based upon an alliance of classes working toward the objectives of socialism and communism. Under this state form, the communists represent but one of several parties and the proletariat one of several surviving social classes, including small proprietors and land holders, all in the process of transition, presumably, to the "higher forms of social development" on the pattern of the Soviet Union. Constitutionally and theoretically this definition was originally an acknowledgement by the Communists of the greater social diversity of the people living under their rule than under the more monolithic (worker, landless peasant) dictatorship of the proletariat in the USSR in the 1930s and hence.

The primacy of the Communist Party in realizing the "basic tasks of the dictatorship of the proletariat" was left to the testimony of everyday events. The concept of a People's Democracy never implied an acquiescence by the Party in the perpetuation of social, economic, and political diversity. It signified rather the construction of socialism and communism from complex social and political conditions.[2]

While the 1952 constitutional system has survived substantially unchanged despite such tremors as de-Stalinization, the return of Gomułka to power, and recently his replacement by Edward Gierek, its uses before and after 1956 have been markedly different. In the latter period, there have been appreciable, though discontinuous, improvements in favor of the rights of legislators and of the individual citizens.

The 1952 Constitution gave legislative power to a one-chamber parliament (Sejm) of 460 members elected every four years, and a Council of State composed of seventeen members elected by the Sejm. The Council includes a chairman (who also fulfills the function of a head of state),* four deputy chairmen, a secretary and eleven ordinary members. The Sejm is a unicameral counterpart of the Supreme Soviet of the USSR. The Sejm is elected on the basis of universal, equal, and direct suffrage of citizens over the age of 18. The Council of State is in some respects a counterpart of the Presidium of the Supreme Soviet in the Russian model. As in the Soviet case, the Polish Council has the power of issuing decrees with the force of laws. It may exercise virtually all legislative powers when the Sejm is not in session. The Council may declare war, proclaim martial law and call a general mobilization. It appoints the Prosecutor General and judges of the Supreme Court as well as the military, diplomatic, and administrative officers; it ratifies

---

*In December 1970, Józef Cyrankiewicz, Premier under Gomułka's regime for some fourteen years, was, in effect, "kicked upstairs" to this post.

international treaties and agreements. It can convoke the Sejm and call national elections, its powers being limited only by the Constitutional provision that the Sejm must meet at least twice a year; that its term may not exceed four years, and by a requirement of *post facto* validation of its decrees by the Sejm. Two of the Council's most significant powers are those of judicial review—the power to interpret laws and to decide conflicts of laws—and the supervision of local government organized in a pyramid of the so-called People's Councils throughout Poland. The Council's judicial functions are exercised on the initiative of the Prosecutor General who is both appointed by and responsible to it. Thus legislative, judicial, and even administrative functions are substantially fused, not separated, in the Polish-Communist parliamentary system.

Typically in 1968, of the seventeen members composing the Council of State, the PZPR directly controlled ten. Among these were three members of the Party's top policy-making body, the Politburo (Spychalski, Loga-Sowiński and Gomułka) and five members of the Party's Central Committee. Of the remaining seven, six were leaders of Parties affiliated wilh the Communists, the Z.S.L. and the S.D. Actually, only one member of the Council, Catholic deputy Jerzy Zawieyski, could be genuinely regarded as independent of the Party. And he was expelled in the latter part of 1968 as Gomułka tightened Party controls.

The traditional executive branch of the government—the Council of Ministers—is appointed and recallable by the Sejm (or the Council of State on behalf of the Sejm). Provisions exist for the enforcement of its responsibility to the legislature through the agencies of interpellation and inquiry, which formally, like the Soviet 1936 model, parallel western democratic practice. Significantly, however, the Council of Ministers is constitutionally defined *not* as a policy making body but as "the highest executive and administrative organ of the state."

In functional terms, the Polish Council of Ministers is much too large and unwieldy to operate continuously as a single, deliberative organ. Its members are, in fact, the chiefs of separate departmental bureaucracies. Their work is planned and coordinated principally through standing and *ad hoc*, interdepartmental committees and subcommittees of the Council of Ministers; in all of these the Prime Minister and the four Deputy Premiers generally exercise special mediating and leadership roles.

The forum in which meaningful discussion of general policy does take place regularly, and in which policy initiatives originate, is the much smaller Politburo of the PZPR. In 1968, this body consisted of eleven full-fledged members and three candidate members, who are entitled to participate in the discussions but do not vote. As shown in Table 2:1, six members of the Politburo, including the Premier, were also members of the Council of Ministers. At the beginning of our "model year," out of thirty-one Ministers, actually twenty-one were high-ranking members of the PZPR, i.e. held positions either in the Party's Politburo, or as members and candidate members of the Party's Central Committee. Only five ministerial posts were held by non-Communists.

The Council of Ministers exercises extensive law-making power by means of decrees; these are subject, routinely, to *post facto* approval of the Sejm.

Up to 1956, the Sejm in Poland represented a mere façade of quasi-democratism traditionally cultivated by all communist regimes. Two-thirds of its members were PZPR deputies; the rest were divided among the United Populist Party (ZSL), the Democratic Party (SD), and those without party affiliations (Bezpartyjni). The overwhelming majority even of the non-communist deputies in that period represented pliant, procommunist front organizations. Moreover, the Sejm rarely met. Most of the legislative and control functions were exercised by the Council of State. Genuine debate or criticism of the regime, its policies, and personnel were never voiced in the Sejm. The Gomułka revolution produced some striking changes and reforms in the all but torpid Polish parliamentarism. Where before 1956 the legislative output was divided into 160 Council of State decrees and just eight laws passed by the whole Sejm, in the next four years the balance was virtually reversed: 114 laws and only twenty-four decrees! The number of plenary sessions of the Sejm after 1956 has risen appreciably. The number of standing legislative committees has been increased from seven to nineteen in 1957.

The preponderance of PZPR deputies has been substantially reduced in the four Sejms elected in 1957, 1961, 1965, and 1969. In the first few years of Gomułka's rule, the Sejm ceased to be a rubber stamp. Government budgets, economic plans, and legislative proposals were subjected to plenary discussion and debate; criticisms, objections, amendments, and "helpful proposals" began to be offered to the Government by individual deputies in the 1960s. Even in plenary meetings some occasional, public criticisms of government actions by a handful of catholic deputies—as in the 1961 Sejm—were voiced. Committee meetings and personal contacts between government officials and legislators had grown more meaningful. Of the hundreds of interpellations and inquiries which the deputies of the Sejm addressed to the

TABLE 2:1 THE COUNCIL OF MINISTERS, FEBRUARY 1968

Members	Portfolio	Party Affiliation
Józef Cyrankiewicz:**	Prime Minister	PZPR
Zenon Nowak:*	Vice Premier	PZPR
Piotr Jaroszewicz:*	Vice Premier	PZPR
Stefan Ignar:	Vice Premier	ZSL
Eugeniusz Szyr:**	Vice Premier and Chairman of the Committee for Science and Technology	PZPR
Franciszek Waniołka:	Vice Premier	PZPR
Adam Rapacki:**	Minister of Foreign Affairs	PZPR
Witold Trąmpczyński:*	Minister of Foreign Trade	PZPR
Marian Spychalski:**	Minister of National Defense	PZPR
Jerzy Albrecht:*	Minister of Finance	PZPR
Jan Mitręga:*	Minister of Mining and Power	PZPR
Janusz Hrynkiewicz:	Minister of Heavy Industry	PZPR
Edward Sznajder:	Minister of Internal Trade	PZPR
Piotr Lewiński:	Minister of Transportation	PZPR
Lucjan Motyka:*	Minister of Culture and Art	PZPR
Roman Gesing:	Minister of Forestry and Timber Industry	ZSL
Henryk Jabłoński:*	Minister of Education and Higher Schools	PZPR
Zygmunt Moskwa:	Minister of Communications	S.D.
Antoni Radliński:*	Minister of Chemical Industry	PZPR
Eugeniusz Stawiński:*	Minister of Light Industry	PZPR
Feliks Pisula:	Minister of Food Industry	ZSL
Mieczysław Jagielski:*	Minister of Agriculture	PZPR
Stanisław Walczac:	Minister of Justice	PZPR

Janusz Burakiewicz:	Minister of Shipping	PZPR
Jerzy Sztachelski:*	Minister of Health and Social Welfare	PZPR
Mieczysław Moczar:*	Minister of Internal Affairs	PZPR
Marian Olewiński:*	Minister of Building and the Building Materials Industry	PZPR
Stanisław Sroka:	Minister of Municipal Economy	PZPR
Stefan Jędrychowski:**	Chairman of the State Commission for Economic Planning	PZPR
Aleksander Burski:	Chairman of the State Committee for Labor and Wages	PZPR
Włodzimierz Lechowicz:	Chairman of the Committee for Small-Scale Industry and Handicraft	SD

* denotes member or candidate member of the Party's Central Committee.

** denotes members and candidate members of the Party's Politburo *or* one of the central control organs of the PZPR, such as the Secretariat and the Party Central Control Commission.

government in recent years most have been answered personally and informally—in the Sejm lobbies and committee rooms. The traditional representative function of taking up constituents' grievances and requests to the administrative organs was revived on a limited scale and quasi-privately. In the case of several bills passed by the Sejm in the early 1960s there had been occasional negative votes and abstentions.[3]

On balance, the Sejm experienced a modest upsurge of influence in the years 1957–1967. But, coincident with Gomułka's anti-Zionist campaign, the invasion of Czechoslovakia, and the mounting repression of dissent, the Sejm suffered an institutional relapse. This situation grew evident in the last years of the 1965 Sejm, and was all but unmistakable in the Sejm elected in the summer of 1969. Ironically, in view of Gomulka's earlier criticism of Stalinist methods, the Sejm was now virtually ignored and kept at arm's length. Given less and less information, its advice was not solicited by the Government: its few independent members were subjected to harassment.

One of the foremost pledges of the new Gierek regime in 1971 was to "revive" the Sejm by genuinely involving it in the formulation of national planning, policy and legislation. It remains to be seen whether the Gierek aspirations of 1971 will prove more successful than Gomułka's in 1956.

Obviously all of the post 1956 reforms fall short of the standards of western parliamentary assemblies. A motion of no confidence in the government has been and is 'unthinkable" in the Polish Sejm. The deputies find no leverage against the government in independent news media, in political parties or, indeed, in honest and competitive elections. Nor can they really regard themselves as personally immune from the Party's vengeance given the role of Polish courts and security police. The changes are indicative, however, of a substantial, even if spasmodic, retreat from a monolithic, one-way, from-the-top-down, Party rule. Gomułka's policies of democratization and relaxation of police controls tended to erode and undermine the monolith of passive acquiescence which characterized both the PZPR and its allies in the so-called Front of National Unity before 1956.

Substantial changes within the political system since 1956 prominently include electoral procedures. To be sure, the Party exercises firm control over all election outcomes through the so-called Front of National Unity (Front Jedności Narodowej—hereafter referred to as the FJN). This organization prepares lists of candidates in both national and local elections. No name appears on the ballot without its authorization.

Illustratively, at the national elections in 1965, the FJN was directed by an executive committee of ten members. The chairman was Edward Ochab, PZPR Politburo member and also Chairman of the Council of State. There were three Vice-Chairmen: Ignacy Loga-Sowiński, member of the PZPR Politburo and head of the official trade union movement; Stanisław Kulczyński, leader of the S.D., and Bolesław Podedworny, a deputy leader of the ZSL. The remaining six committee members, titled "secretaries," included two high ranking representatives of the ZSL, one from the SD, and three from the PZPR, including Witold Jarosiński, of the Party's Central Committee. Thus the FJN was securely directed by an elite of the Party and of its principal collaborators as well. But the applications of PZPR power have changed.

In 1946 the Communists staged a referendum asking Polish voters to support them in the abolition of the Senate, the nationalization of industry, the carrying out of land reform, and the annexation of the western territories from Germany. The results of that poll, where the Communists obtained affirmative responses ranging from 66.2 percent on the abolition of the Senate to 94.2 percent of the electorate on the Oder-Neisse line, were heavily falsified. The subsequent election of 1947, in which the Government Bloc crushed Milołajczyk's

TABLE 2:2 PARTY DISTRIBUTION IN THE POLISH SEJM, 1952–1965

	1952		1957		1961		1965		1969	
	Seats	*%*	*Seats*	*%*	*Seats*	*%*	*Seats*	*%*	*Seats*	*%*
PZPR	273	64.2	239	52.1	256	55.7	255	55.4	255	55.4
ZSL	90	21.2	118	25.7	117	25.4	117	25.4	117	25.4
SD	25	5.9	39	8.5	39	8.5	39	8.5	39	8.5
Non-Party	37	8.7	63	13.7	48	10.4	49	10.7	49	10.7
Total	425	100.0	459	100.0	460	100.0	460	100.0	460	100.0

opposition and claimed over 80 percent of popular support, was characterized by terrorism, intimidation, and mass falsification of the actual results.[4]

The election of 1952 provided virtually no choice to the Polish voter inasmuch as the electoral ordinance passed by the Sejm that year provided for only one candidate per each parliamentary seat to be filled. Nominations were limited to the safely Communist and Communist-led "mass organizations." Voters could not write in names of their own choice. They could, conceivably, cross out the candidates' names on the ballot; if any candidate's name had been crossed off by 50 percent of the voters, a subsequent by-election would have to fill the seat. However, not one seat needed to be so filled in 1952. The Party's Front of National Unity was officially credited with the support of over 99 percent of the electorate. While even in this election falsification of results may well have been employed, the presence of officials and security agents discouraged people from secret voting (booths were provided *optionally* for those who wanted to use them). Most persons simply dropped the ballots in the urns as soon as they had received them—in full view, naturally, of the ubiquitous security police!

Gomułka brought about a significant change which made the election of 1957 much more than a sham even if it was still very much less than the western practice.[5] According to a law of October 26, 1956 universal secrecy of voting was restored and the number of candidates could exceed the available seats by a ratio of up to two-thirds. Actually, there were 750 candidates for the 460 Sejm seats in the 1957 election and only about one-half of the candidates were PZPR members. Voters could cross off names they did not like; they could not write in their own suggestions. No candidate whose name was crossed off by more than 50 percent of the voters could be elected. Thus, even if the choice for the average voter was not between a Communist or an anti-Communist it was at least possible in some districts to show one's displeasure by voting non-Communist or to accord Communist candidates the lowest public ranking.* In 1957 the PZPR claimed only 51.7 percent of the seats in the Sejm, the balance going to several Communist approved groupings. In 1960, the Party again somewhat tightened the electoral law by decreasing available choices. Only 616 candidates were allowed to stand on the ballot for the Sejm in the 1961 election and 630 in 1965 and 1969. The ratio of Communist candidates was

---

*In no election since 1957 have the voters of any district rejected the *whole* FJN ticket. We may keep in mind that time spent in the voting booth is still subject to an obviously negative interpretation by the security police.

increased in these elections to a point where even a nominal non-Communist majority would have been impossible from the outset. Nevertheless, the Polish electoral system now provides the regime with something more than a ritual. It has made it possible to gauge the mood of the people in response to the policies of the regime. In 1965, Poland's Premier Józef Cyrankiewicz was publicly rebuked in his particular constituency, having polled the lowest vote among the several candidates elected from his district. The Polish Marxist sociologist Jerzy J. Wiatr has described Polish elections since 1965 as being "consent elections." He has contrasted this concept at one extreme with "safe elections" in which the voter has virtually no choice of candidates and in which "the power of the ruling forces is not challenged from any side"; at the other extreme are competitive elections with clear-cut ballot choices on the western model. In contra-distinction to these, Wiatr has described Polish elections as contests in which: ". . . the voter does not make any choice between parties competing for power, but: (1) he is personally free to express his acceptance or disapproval of the governmental policy with the assumption that his vote would have some meaning for future policy; (2) he can influence the selection of the members of representative bodies both in negative and positive way (by voting against some and/or for some other candidates). The consent elections do not decide who will rule the country, but they influence the way in which the country will be ruled."[6]

After the proportional representation system inherited from pre-war Poland was abolished, following the 1947 election, the country was divided into sixty-seven constituencies with the number of parliamentary seats in each proportional to the population and varying from three to seven. Since 1957, the number of candidates per constituency has varied from five to eleven, giving the voters some positive choice among candidates. In cases where voters do not cross off names, the candidates are elected in the order in which the FJN has presented their names on the ballot. J. J. Wiatr concluded in a 1962 study that, both in terms of electoral participation and the crossing of PZPR candidates off the ballots, the regime has found the most support in the newly settled western territories of Poland. Urban areas have also tended to be more pro-regime than rural ones, though differences have not been very sharp, according to Wiatr. He also found that on a nation-wide basis the names of Communist party candidates were crossed off most often, followed by the candidates of the Peasant Party (ZSL), the Democrats (SD) and those without party affiliation in that order. A Communist himself, Wiatr explains the phenomenon as a voter's natural reaction, in venting grievances against those identified as the main power-holders.

Already in 1954, according to Wiatr, local elections to the People's Councils constituted a transition from "safe" to "consent" elections. That year 18.4 percent of the candidates presented by the FJN were replacements of those criticized at pre-election voters' meetings. Actually, such meetings have been used at once as platforms for government campaign propaganda and as sounding boards gauging popular responses to candidates and to issues. The procedures followed do not involve voting by the people attending. Instead, the managers of the FJN profess to secure "a sense of the meeting" from such criticism and discussion as may take place. According to Wiatr, the FJN removed roughly three out of four candidates who had been "objected to" in the pre-election meetings of 1954. Obviously, the total concession to popular demands thus involved was still quite small. The substitutes chosen in place of the rejected candidates were not popular choices but simply yet another set of National Front nominees. The Party, of course, does not make any bones about its determination to hold on to power. It seeks to discover and identify itself with popular opinion, however, and is anxious to increase its face to face contacts with the electorate or alternatively "the masses."

This was also clearly evident in the national parliamentary elections of 1965 and 1969. The experiences in the pre-election "consultative" meetings with voters have been widely discussed in the PZPR chief ideological organ, *Nowe Drogi*. Party secretaries in various sections of the country vied with one another in organizing mass meetings, with claims of popular participation running into hundreds of thousands attending, and large percentages of these taking part in the discussions and question-and-answer sessions. The party's election post-mortems indicate that its leaders have been obviously concerned to affect solicitude for voters' objections to particular candidates. There has also been a more genuine effort to air popular grievances and concerns than was the case in the past.

Thus, in 1965 a PZPR secretary in the Gdańsk province reported, predictably, popular concern with "American aggression in Vietnam and the Dominican Republic" but there were other, obviously genuine, themes which he also uncovered. For example, the voters demanded more equitable distribution of essential consumer goods, an end to shortages, and more and better service from the bureaucratic apparatus in charge of the Polish economy. The Gdańsk Party secretary seemed to be affected by the dialogue no less than the voters and concluded that the red tape, delays, hostile attitudes, and inefficiency of the bureaucracy were the real and as yet unsolved demands of the electorate. A Warsaw Party secretary reported the housing shortage as the single most important issue, followed by demands for: improvement of municipal transportation; end to bureaucratic obstructions; further democratization of Polish life; increased attention to public order and security in the city suburbs; better education for the youth; improvement in the distribution of goods; raising of wages and incomes.[7]

Since 1957 the membership of the Sejm has changed without becoming generally more representative of the Polish people at large. There has been a significant increase of better educated deputies, but also a decrease in the number of women parliamentarians, and, perhaps most anomalously, a growing "generation gap" between the Sejm and the population at large.

In the 1952–1956 Sejm, dominated by the PZPR, 39.7 percent of the deputies had not gone beyond a primary-level education. In the Sejm elected in 1957 only 18.5 percent of the deputies were in that category; in 1961 only 17.0 percent; and in 1965, 20.0 percent. The share of deputies who had completed secondary education and have had some higher education rose from 21.9 percent in 1952 to 33.6 and 34.0 percent, respectively, in 1957 and 1961. It was 29.3 percent in the 1965 Sejm. The share of those with completed university education rose from 32.0 in 1952 to 39.9, 42.0, and 41.6 percent in the three subsequent national elections.

The number of women deputies declined in both absolute and relative terms between 1952 and 1965, from 74 (17.4 percent) to 57 (12.0 percent). It is noteworthy that in the general Polish population, women still outnumber men, although the gap has been narrowing in recent years. According to a 1966 census, some 53 percent of the Polish population consisted of people under the age of 30. But with respect to the age of deputies, the Polish parliament has grown increasingly unrepresentative of its constituency. In the Sejm of 1952 deputies under 30 accounted for 7.5 percent of the membership. Those under 40 accounted for 33.9 percent. In 1957, however, deputies under 30 declined to 4.1 percent; those under 40 to 27.1 percent. In 1961, the figures were 2.6 and 24.6 percent respectively. In 1965, the Sejm became even older with 2.7 percent under the age of 30 and only 17.7 percent under 40. Actually, the present parliament had the largest representation yet of those over 50 and those over 60. It seems that the significant aging of Poland's parliamentarians reflects the regime's inability—all its reforms notwithstanding—to recruit politically reliable elements among the youth, both for the PZPR and for its "fronts" or affiliates.*

In local government, the People's Councils have been an important instrument of Communist rule under the Gomułka regime. From their inception in 1950 they represented an attempt to identify local government with a wide measure of popular self-rule. Constitutionally, the whole network of these Councils has represented a delegation of power and responsibility from the center rather than residual autonomy on a federal model. The Councils represent on the highest level the seventeen principal provinces or *województwa* of Poland and the largest cities like Warsaw, Poznań, Kraków and Łódź. They descend down to county, precinct, and even village levels. Each council is elected by direct popular vote at the appropriate level of government from joint lists of candidates submitted by the FJN and comparable to the Sejm elections.

In 1965 over 170,000 persons served on these Councils. One interesting difference between local and national representation in Poland has been the dilution of PZPR strength at local levels. Where in the Sejm the percentage of Communist members has never fallen below an absolute majority, it has ranged between only 40 and 46 percent since 1958 in local representation as a whole. In terms of different levels of government, the PZPR has assured itself a degree of dominance roughly proportional to the significance of the particular Council. In the provincial Councils PZPR membership has remained safely above 50 percent. At precinct levels it has sometimes fallen below one-third and significant representation has been given to non-party elements and the peasant group, ZSL.

The Councils have acted both as representatives of their communities and as organs of the central government. They have operated under a system of "democratic centralism" where the decisions of all higher level Councils are binding on all lower ones. The ultimate authority has always been lodged in the Council of State which can set aside any decisions, rulings or ordinances rendered locally. The executive functions of the Councils have been carried out—on the central model—by their Presidia. The Presidia, in turn, have absorbed and developed a large local bureaucracy of their own. In 1966, some 127,-000 functionaries were employed by them. As with the Sejm so with the Councils, the importance of the popular legislative and deliberative organs (as opposed to the executive-administrative presidia) has tended to increase after 1956. The Councils oversee—and subject to

---

*Analogous data for the Sejm elected in 1969 was not available.

the consent and supremacy of the central authorities—control and regulate a whole spectrum of social, economic and cultural activities within their territorial limits. They are the legal "owners" of most of the public facilities like schools, shops, restaurants, hospitals, and clinics within their areas. They control the supply of such public services, as water, gas, electricity, and transportion; they control public health, sanitation, welfare and insurance schemes. The Councils share in a variety of tax proceeds in their districts (which they help to collect), while a substantial part of their work (about half) is subsidized by grants from the central government. One of the more important functions of the Councils is an across-the-board power of complaints and appeals (ultimately to the Council of State) with respect to any governmental or other activity within their territorial confines. They thus provide a grass-roots sounding board for the regime.

Certain crucial areas of political and economic life, however, remain altogether outside their regulatory powers—the armed forces, the security police and the citizens' militia, mining and larger industrial plants, the larger state farms, railroads, postal services, and among cultural institutions, the universities. Nevertheless, the Councils have offered some welcome relief from the uniform regulation of everyday life by the central authorities in Warsaw. In recent years, the Councils have attempted to provide more variety of entertainment and consumer services to the people. And the Party's hold on these Councils has also been appreciably looser.

Some recent data show that of the 171,724 persons who have been elected to them in 1965, the PZPR has only 46.8 percent of the total; the Peasant Party (ZSL) is next with 21.6 percent of the Councillors; the Democratic Party (SD) has only 2.5 percent and the remainder of nearly 30 percent do not have any party affiliation. The ZSL is represented in the rural areas and the SD in the predominantly urban. The party line-ups in the People's Councils in 1965 and 1969 were substantially the same as those in 1961, just as has been the case with the distribution of seats in the Sejm.

On the other hand, there has been a significant shift in the occupational profile among the People's Councillors since the first "post-Gomułka" election of 1958. Workers' representation has remained remarkably constant and surprisingly low; it was 11.7 percent in 1958; 13.3 in 1961 and 12.3 in 1965. But the representation of peasants has declined form 53.2 percent in 1958 to 44.8 percent in 1965 while those classified as white collar workers increased from 28.4 to 37.1 percent. Even in the larger cities the average worker representation remains below 30 percent, with the high in Poznań, where 37.3 percent of the

Councillors are workers. The recent changes seem to reflect the increasing dominance of managerial elements in the PZPR itself.[8]

In addition to such relatively traditional political institutions as the Sejm, the Council of Ministers or local government People's Councils, the formulation and execution of public policy in Poland is also the province of new economic organizations. At the top level is the Planning Commission of the Council of Ministers.[9] This organization is charged with the formulation of the state's over-all economic policies and with the formulation of measures designed to effectuate them. Legally its powers are only advisory. The powers of implementation are vested in the Council of Ministers and the appropriate People's Council. In practice the body's "recommendations" have been frequently also "decisions," particularly before Gomułka's return to power. The Commission has maintained a professional staff of about 1,000 persons in recent years. After 1956, considerable influence in the Planning Commission had been exercised by professional economists who, like the late Professor Oskar Lange, Stefan Kurowski, or Edward Lipiński have represented "unorthodox" Marxian thinking, highly critical of the regimentation, and excessive centralization practiced during the pre-1956 period in Poland. On the other hand, one of the changes initiated by the Gomułka regime has been to accentuate the Council's advisory rather than decision-making role. Thus, a reform which in 1956 was regarded as "liberal" in that it took power away from "faceless bureaucrats behind the scenes" has traveled full circle into the sixties. Just as the Commission has tended to become more open and liberal in its views, its powers have declined in favor of the more orthodox membership of the Council of Ministers.

In November 1956, parts of the management and planning functions in the Polish economy came under the direction of the Workers' Councils. Initially, these Councils, representative of employees, were to share—with state appointed directors—in the management of individual economic enterprises. Wage levels, profit-sharing, and work rules, as well as more general technical and financial problems of industry, were placed within the decision-making power of the Councils. But the Workers' Councils had proved so demanding and difficult to control that the regime was forced to reorganize the system. In 1959 so-called Conferences of Worker-Self-Government absorbed the Workers' Councils as the regime's grass roots "partners" in the running of the economy. One effect of this change has been to dilute the impact of actual worker participation in economic decision-making. The Conferences include in each plant not only Workers' Councils' but also additional representatives from the official trade unions, the

PZPR, the factory council (management), and technical or scientific personnel of the so-called NOT (Naczelna Organizacja Techniczna or Chief Technical Organization). Depending on whether the particular enterprise is an industrial or agricultural one, either the ZMS (Związek Młodzieży Socjalistycznej or Association of Socialist Youth) or the ZMW (Związek Młodzieży Wiejskiej or Association of Rural Youth) is also generally represented. The dilution of worker participation in local economic decisions has been combined with strengthened Party control. The process has been illustrative of the Party's hold, both in economic and political spheres, exercised by means of overlapping influence in interdependent organizations.

Since 1959 the number of plants covered by Worker Self-Government Conferences has steadily declined from 11,408 in 1959, to 8,751 in 1966. The number of annual meetings, or actual "conferences," has also fallen from 40.6 to some 36 thousand. In 1966, the total official membership of Worker Self-Government Conferences was 233,706. The share of actual plant employees, represented by Workers' Councils, was only 91,036. Even of these nearly 22.7 thousand were classified as engineering-technical employees, as distinguished from "workers." In an economy in which women and young people predominate, the officially manipulated Workers' Councils now include only about 12 percent of members who are under 30 and even fewer women. Dissatisfaction and opposition have been muffled by official misrepresentation.

An important development of the "December Revolution" of 1970 was a revival of authentic worker representation on an *ad hoc* basis. Polish strikers in Łódź, Gdańsk, Gdynia, and Szczecin had told the Party leaders of their grievances, directly, repeatedly, and in no uncertain terms. It would be premature to speculate, however, whether the meetings held between workers, workers' representatives, and the Party officials in the winter of 1970–71 would, in fact, lead to more representative union organizations in the future. Would they lead to an institutionalized dialogue between the workers and the Party? The Gierek-Jaroszewicz leadership was clearly solicitous of worker claims during the height of the crisis following the ouster of Gomułka. It listened patiently to demands for higher wages, a revised bonus-incentive system, more and better housing, consumer goods, and fringe benefits. Confronted by massive strike actions in many industries, it tried to "talk its way" out of the economic breakdown thus engendered. Yet, many of its appointments to union and government posts understandably raised worker apprehensions. Heretofore, the role of unions and Worker Self-Government Conferences had been clearly supportive of Party economic policies and the December upheaval has not yet brought any institutional changes.

One of the chief means of consolidating power and advancing Party political objectives has been a reshaping of the Polish judiciary. Until the passage of the Judiciary Act of 1950, the Communists made changes in the legal system in a piecemeal, sometimes even haphazard fashion.

The Party in Poland did not need to fight against a long judicial tradition based on case law, as in the Anglo-Saxon systems, or against court powers of judicial review as specifically in the American system. The prewar Polish legal order was based on statutory laws which, once properly promulgated, were binding on the courts. The decisions of higher courts were binding on the lower ones in specific cases, not generally. Enactments of legislative and presidential decrees were not subject to judicial veto. On the other hand, the independence and the impartiality of the courts were constitutionally safeguarded under all the pre-1939 regimes, and the safeguards were variously buttressed by the administration and organization of the courts. The appointments, promotions and transfers of judges required the nominations and the consent of the judges themselves in conjunction with action by the Minister of Justice. As set out by the Judiciary Act of 1928, judges could be appointed only from among those meeting stringent legal-professional requirements; their decisions were not subject to review or veto by any non-judicial organs. They could not be removed from office except on conviction by courts. The remuneration and control of the judiciary were carried on separately from all other administrative personnel of the state, with carefully spelled out legal safeguards and the actual participation or substantial self-government by the judges themselves. The judges themselves were forbidden to affiliate with political parties or publicly take part in partisan politics.* The police and the public prosecutor's office were legally barred from any control over the courts.

In general similarity with many western and particularly the French systems, Polish prewar courts had the power to protect the interests of individuals against bureaucratic abuse, whether in the form of a

---

*From 1918 until the Piłsudski *coup* of 1926 the independence of Polish courts was not merely the letter of the law but substantially also the practice. Such shortcomings as existed in the administration of Polish justice could not be attributed to direct government pressure upon or control of the judiciary. After 1926 this was on the whole less true. Polish justice was unquestionably undermined by police methods, and detention camps like Bereza-Kartuska which became more and more important after 1930. Even during this period, however, the abuses stemmed less from any misuse of courts than from their non-use.

misapplication of legislative enactments or other illegal behavior on the part of government personnel. Since 1922 a Supreme Administrative Tribunal handled such cases. The Communist regime gradually overturned and subverted this system of justice to its own purposes, although in 1944 it began its rule by professing allegiance to the old liberal constitutional system of 1921. Even before the enactment of the law of 1950 regulating the judiciary, and the Constitution of 1952, the concept of "legality" as something reflecting a fair and impartial administration of the laws by the courts was being superseded by the new concepts of a "people's legality" and "socialist legality." These required an unmistakable partisan subjectivity on the part of judges and courts, calling upon them to be conscious instruments of party policy and active promoters of the new socio-political order in Poland. Communist-oriented political vigilantes, not learned and impartial lawyers, became the prized leaders of the new legal system. In Marxian terms, justice became the conscious servant of the working people's interests. It shed its bourgeois "hypocritical mask of objectivity." The guidance in discerning the "working people's interests," and applying or using the law accordingly, came naturally enough from the workers' vanguard—the Communist Party. In the 1940's many prewar laws were simply ruled null and void by Communist courts. Law was at the convenience of the Party, which gave virtually open directives to the courts on matters of judicial policy and conduct. As Peter Siekanowicz noted:[10]

". . . even speeches delivered by the leaders of the Party were treated as directives for the courts in the administration of justice. Legal periodicals discussed them and established the ways in which the courts had to apply them. They were also discussed at judicial conferences. In addition, the government administration issued orders on the enforcement of the resolutions passed by the Party. In this way the resolutions of the party were *extra legem* [and] made an additional factual source of law to be respected by the courts in their decisions. Any violation of these resolutions might be understood as a violation of either the people's legality or of the interests of the state as they are understood by the Party."

The Party promoted a theory of "social" rather than "narrowly legal" interpretation of statutes for the guidance of the courts. The social purposes of laws, their impact on class interests, and the "will of the masses" were urged upon the judiciary as significant interpretive considerations.

The judiciary's independence and security of tenure were effectively destroyed by a variety of methods. One of these was the creation of special tribunals, including military ones, which tried certain types of cases outside the ordinary structure of the courts. This was true even in cases involving civilians, under very broadly defined categories of crime such as "Offenses Against Public Security and the Public Order," and "Offenses Against the Economic Interests of State." The charge of collaboration with the Nazis and of "cooperation with Fascist underground organizations" offered a particularly fertile field for essentially political purge trials. In many of these during the 1940s and early 1950s, virtually the whole proceedings and even the identity of the courts remained secret. The remaining Polish courts of the basically traditional variety, i.e., the districts and the provincial courts were gradually restaffed with Communist trainees and their independence severely restricted.

Under the Act of 1950 the informal practices of the previous few years were codified. Judges were not merely encouraged but by law required to show political bias as "revolutionary constructors of a socialist society." On the other hand, the Minister of Justice was empowered to waive all legal and educational criteria in appointing them to office. Although the 1952 Constitution made provision for the popular election of judges, no legislation or administrative action has subsequently implemented this, so that judicial office still remains (except in the case of the Supreme Court named by the Council of State) as the gift of the Minister of Justice. Moreover, the pre-1939 protection of judicial tenure, revokable solely upon legal conviction, has been set aside. The Minister can remove, demote, or transfer judges as easily and arbitrarily as any other state bureaucrats. Judicial salaries, set at rather low levels (ranging from 2000 to 4500 zlotys in mid-1960s), enjoy no statutory protection against government manipulation.

The regular courts in People's Poland currently consist of three principal hierarchies: 320 county or district courts (sądy powiatowe); nineteen regional or provincial courts (sądy wojewódzkie), and the Supreme Court (Sąd Najwyższy) at the apex of the pyramid. The Supreme Court considers all appeals emanating from the regional and district courts. Its members are appointed for five year terms by the Council of State and submit annual reports to the Council. The Court is actually composed of four separate branches or "chambers"; one for civil cases; one for criminal cases; a chamber for labor and social welfare appeals, and a military affairs chamber; a total of 104 judges serve in these four branches of the Supreme Court.

Since the Communist regime faced an obvious dearth of personnel upon taking power in the 1944–45 period, it was willy-nilly forced to rely upon substantial members of prewar judiciary. Of 3109 judges before 1939 over thirty percent were exterminated or died during World War II. Of the remainder, the Communists hired more than half (1,346) almost immediately, and by February 1946 additional judges were qualified by the Minister of Justice to serve on a "temporary" basis. In 1950 as a result of these measures, and, notwithstanding apparently intensive efforts to train new personnel, 59.3 percent of Poland's prewar judges were back on the bench. In 1954 the number declined to 26 percent and by 1956 (seventeen years after the outbreak of the war) it was only 17.8 percent of the total body of Polish judges.

The regime has attempted to minimize potential vulnerabilities resulting from such heavy reliance on prewar personnel by introducing so-called "assessors" into the legal system. Before 1939 laymen served in Polish regular courts only in the traditional capacity of jurors in criminal proceedings. They participated in decision making of the special labor and commercial courts to which they were nominated by labor and professional groups. Since 1950, however, laymen have become part of the judicial machinery in all the courts of original jurisdiction: the district courts and the provincial courts. Unlike jurors, the assessors do not confine their participation to passing on the facts of the case; they share in the whole plethora of judicial functions from interrogation of witnesses in court to the passing of sentence. Two assessors and a judge compose each of the regular courts, save for the Supreme Court which is wholly professional. The assessors can, if they are so disposed, dominate the proceedings. In all decisions, on facts or law, majority rule is invoked. According to the statute, the assessors are periodically elected by the People's Councils of their respective counties or provinces. In practice, they are generally chosen by the five-member, party-dominated Presidia of these Councils. The criteria of selection followed since 1950 stress the choice of persons "devoted to the building of socialism in Poland" by virtue of their class origins ("kulaks" and "speculators" have been excluded) and their party affiliations or political participation. Legal and educational criteria have been generally deemphasized. Provincial and district courts make annual reports of their activities to their respective People's Councils.

The impact of the assessors on the courts in Poland has been mixed and, in some respects, contradictory. In certain cases, assessors have been elected who have not shown even a minimal interest in the work of the courts. One result has been the delay of judicial proceedings because of assessor absenteeism. Another typical result has been the continued dominance of professional judges, flanked by assessors whose ability and interests have made it impossible for them seriously to affect or participate in the business of the courts. In many cases, however, Party activists, elected as assessors, have succeeded in dominating the courts, frequently with little regard for western notions of due process of law, the rights of participants, or any of the most elementary requirements of the law.

Under Communist rule, the Polish courts have been rendered virtually powerless to protect citizens from abuse by government officials. The latter can no longer be sued by ordinary citizens. At most, citizens may lodge complaints against administrative maltreatment either with the Prosecutor General's office or directly with the agency which aggrieved them. Any relief or compensation is wholly at the discretion of the government. As a consequence of the 1950 reforms, the Prosecutor General's office had not only taken over the function of chief public prosecutor on behalf of the government, as in prewar days, but also that of overseer of "socialist legality" throughout the whole structure of government and society. In practice, this has made the Prosecutor General's office the supervisor of the courts and the dominant party in proceedings initiated by it. Prosecution demands, however harsh, have rarely been questioned or opposed by the judges. Warrants of arrest and preliminary investigations preceding trials have become the province of the Prosecutor General's office. The Prosecutor General, in turn, has been the appointee of the Council of State and invariably a high ranking PZPR official. In common with Soviet practice, the Prosecutor General's independence of the Minister of Justice, has given the party a system of multiple and counter checking means for fact-finding and control, with ultimate responsibility neither to the Council of State nor to the Government but to the highest organs of the Party itself.

Before 1956, the powers of the Prosecutor General's office in the field of arrests, interrogations, and detention of suspects were exercised more often by the Security Police than by government attorneys. This aspect of Polish justice constituted probably the darkest single page of Polish Stalinism. The police, under the Ministry of Public Security, were a law unto themselves. Arrests were often carried on without the knowledge, let alone consent, of judicial authorities; people were detained in secrecy for indefinite periods and frequently subjected to medieval tortures such as the tearing out of fingernails, beatings, freezings, floggings, and the like. Confessions were suitably "manufactured." Since virtually no one could be sure when, where, and how the Security Police might strike next, the system served the totalitarian purpose of pulverizing and undermining all potential as well as actual opposition, and virtually all forms of social association. Even the Party itself was not a privileged sanctuary. Ultimate control over the police was exercised by the PZPR Politburo Commision for Security Matters, one of whose members was the "Polish Beria,"

Stanisław Radkiewicz. Until Stalin's demise the operations of the Polish police appear to have been influenced by directives and pressures from top ranking Soviet leaders, including on occasion both Beria and Stalin.[11]

The October 1956 revolution ushered in changes and improvements in the judicial system, moderating some of the worst abuses, though the changes have not been institutionally sweeping. Top ranking officials responsible for the earlier "reign of terror," including the Minister of Justice, the Prosecutor General, the Minister of Internal Security and the Chief Justice of the Supreme Court were dismissed. A mass amnesty for those imprisoned for political crimes was carried through, involving at least 35,000 persons. Party organs carried on for the first time a discussion of improper pressures which, it was admitted, had been brought to bear on the judiciary. Disclosures of at least some of the crimes of the 1944–1956 period were made. Among those punished, Roman Romkowski, Deputy Minister of Security was sentenced to fifteen years' imprisonment; two of the principal police investigators, Fejgin and Różański, received twelve- and fourteen-year sentences respectively. The Ministry of State Security was abolished, and some of the investigative and police work divided between the Ministers of Justice, Interior, and the Prosecutor General's office. Increased professional qualifications for both judges and assessors have been enacted into law.

In order to remove the glaring and obvious inadequacies of the legal system, the Party has somewhat modified its approach to "socialist legality." Direct, gross pressure upon judges and courts has been denounced and ascribed to Stalinist excesses. The Party has *not* renounced, however, the concept of judicial subjectivity based on the "class interests of the working people." In recent years it has emphasized, instead, an indirect and general education of the judiciary through Marxist—Leninist indoctrination. Thus, the Party tacitly admits that even "class justice" must possess a degree of impartiality and general applicability if it is to be accepted and respected.

Among the most important demands faced by the new Gierek regime has been that for representativeness in the Polish institutions; for trade unions and workers' councils that would genuinely reflect the aspirations of the rank and file; for courts which would observe due process and show respect for public opinion; for student associations independent of the Party; for a Sejm which could genuinely control and criticize the government. Whether the Party's self-interest would allow far-reaching reforms of such a legacy of institutional lock-step remains to be seen.

NOTES

1. The only formal constitutional change since the Gomułka Revolution has been the expansion of the Council of State from fifteen to seventeen members.

2. On the theory of "People's Democracy" see Paul E. Zinner, *National Communism and Popular Revolt in Eastern Europe* (New York, 1956), chapter 1. Cf. R. A. Rosa, "The Soviet Theory of People's Democracy," *World Politics*, vol. I, no. 4, July 1949, pp. 489–510.

3. On the revival of Polish parliamentarism under Gomułka's rule see Vincent C. Chrypiński, "Legislative Committees in Polish Lawmaking," *Slavic Review*, vol. XXV, no. 2, June 1966, pp. 247–258.

4. See particularly the accounts of Arthur Bliss-Lane, *op. cit.*, 276–288; S. Korboński, *Warsaw in Chains* (New York, 1959), pp. 185–198; and S. Mikołajczyk's *Rape of Poland, op. cit.*, pp. 145–202.

5. See. Z. A. Pełczynski, "Poland 1957," in D. E. Butler (ed.) *Elections Abroad* (London, 1959).

6. See J. J. Wiatr, "Elections and Voting Behavior in Poland," in A. Ranney, (ed.) *Essays on the Behavioral Study of Politics* (Urbana, 1962), p. 239 and pp. 235–251, *passim.*

7. See Ptasiński, Szydlak and Kępa in *Nowe Drogi*, vol. 7, no. 194, July 1965, pp. 44–62.

8. See H. Olszewski and J. Surmanczyński, "Radni Kadencji 1965–1969 w Liczbach," *Nowe Drogi*, vol. 8, no. 195, August 1965, pp. 190–99. See also H. Stehle, *The Independent Satellite* (New York, 1966), pp. 188–191 on the expanded role of the Councils recently.

9. On this subject see J. M. Montias, *Central Planning in Poland* (New Haven, 1962); Jiri Kilaja, *A Polish Factory: A Case Study of Workers Participation in Decision Making* (Lexington, Ky., 1960).

10. V. Gsovski and K. Grzybowski, *Government, Law and Courts in the Soviet Union and Eastern Europe* (New York, 1959), vol. I, chapter 24, pp. 732–33. See also Grzegorz Leopold Seidler, "Marxist Legal Thought in Poland," *Slavic Review*, vol. XXVI, no. 3, September 1967, pp. 382–394; Joseph C. Gidynski, "Private Property Rights to Dwelling Houses in Post-War Poland," *The Polish Review*, vol. VII, no. 1, winter 1962, pp. 3–35; Aleksander W. Rudzinski, "Sovietization of Civil Law in Poland," *Slavic Review*, vol. XV, February 1956, pp. 216–243.

11. On this subject see the testimony of Jozef Światło, former security police official who defected to the West in *News from Behind the Iron Curtain*, Free Europe Committee, Inc., New York, March 1955.

3

The Ruling Party
and Its Adjuncts

THE PRINCIPAL POLICY-MAKING role in Poland belongs neither to the Council of Ministers nor to the Council of State. It is lodged in the ruling Communist Party (PZPR).[1] The Party was founded as the KPP (Komunistyczna Partia Polski) in December 1918 primarily as a result of a merger between the Social Democratic Party of the Kingdom of Poland and Lithuania (SDKPiL) and the extreme leftwing of the Polish Socialist Party (PPS). The KPP was made up of those who hoped for and expected an imminent expansion of the Russian revolution westward into Poland and Germany and who, unlike most Polish socialists, were willing to subordinate considerations of national independence to the objective of a radical and thorough social revolution on an international scale.

For reasons touched on in Chapter I, the Party continued a very marginal popular force in Polish politics until its dissolution by Stalin in 1938.[2] The highest membership claim made by the KPP in the interwar years was approximately twelve thousand. Except for a smattering of deputies in the Polish parliament, its leaders operated in underground secrecy throughout the 1930's.

Between 1938 and 1942—i.e. between the demise of the allegedly compromised, Trotskyite, and spy-riddled KPP, and the emergence of the Polish Workers Party (PPR)—virtually all of the old-time Polish Communist leaders had perished. Some were "liquidated" by the Russians as "deviationists"; others met the same fate at the hands of the Nazis. At the conclusion of the War, the new Communist leaders were men almost wholly unknown to the Polish public at large. Names like "Bierut" and "Gomułka," "Radkiewicz" or "Minc" were just as mysterious to most Poles in 1944–45 as they would be or might have been to most Americans. The most prominent among the new leadership

48

were Władysław Gomułka and Bolesław Bierut.

The man who dominated Polish Communism during the period of Stalin's rule and after, until his own death, was Bolesław Bierut (1892–1956). Bierut was illustrative of the so-called Muscovite element in the Polish Communist movement. Since 1919 when he joined the original KPP, Bierut probably spent more time in the Soviet Union and abroad then he did in Poland. He worked for the Comintern in Moscow and participated in various international missions as its agent. He was arrested in 1933 in Poland and sentenced to a seven year jail term, but when war broke out he managed to escape to the USSR, where he was clearly accorded greater confidence by Stalin than any other Polish Communist. Bierut did not return to Poland until 1943, reportedly parachuted behind German lines. He successively served as Chairman of the KRN in Nazi-occupied Poland and then of the PKWN in Soviet-occupied Lublin. Between 1947 and 1952 Bierut served as President of Poland and simultaneously General Secretary of the PZPR after Gomułka's ouster in 1948. From 1952 until 1954 he served as Premier, having relinquished the Presidency. He kept the Party leadership until his death in Moscow in March 1956, following the dramatic Twentieth Soviet Communist Party Congress in which Khrushchev exposed some of the crimes of the Stalin era. Bierut had been Stalin's principal "trusted man" in Poland and generally regarded as the Polish version of the selfsame "cult of personality." His death marked the end of the Stalinist phase of Polish Communism.

In the immediate post war period Gomułka and Bierut represented two wings and two orientations in the Communist movement. Their divergence did not become generally obvious until Tito's breach with Moscow in 1948.[4] The first orientation was that of native communism made up of men who, like Gomułka, had spent most of their lives in Poland, advanced in Party ranks through services rendered at home, who remembered and obviously resented Stalin's harsh treatment of Polish Communists and his pitiless sacrifice of the whole Polish movement to the exigencies of Soviet foreign policy. These Communists were relatively nationalistic; their attitude to the Soviets was based upon a realistic appreciation of the need for continued Soviet support against the Polish Party's domestic and foreign adversaries. It was not based primarily upon sentimental or world-revolutionary considerations, nor upon the kind of personal subservience to Moscow which characterized leaders without any appreciable following at home. Gomułka and his supporters believed that, with Soviet help, and under a guarantee of Soviet alliance, Polish Communism should be free to adapt Marxian postulates of social and economic development in accordance with the specific conditions of contemporary Poland. In abstract terms, this was all perfectly orthodox Leninist doctrine. Practically, however, Stalin considered devotion to Soviet interests and to the Soviet socio-political example as the *sine qua non* of Communist orthodoxy.

Bierut both led and symbolized the Party's Muscovite wing with which Stalin hoped not merely to make Poland a communist state but a *de facto* extension of the Soviet Union. In the Muscovites' perspective the primacy of the USSR expressed in the wishes of the Kremlin was all important. Poland was merely part of a larger design engineered by Stalin and the Soviet leadership. The Muscovites, like Red Army Marshal Rokossovsky, were frequently more Russian than Polish in their personal backgrounds and generally, like Bierut, owed their careers and positions directly to Soviet favor and designation rather than to the indigeneous rank-and-file.

Gomułka, who was born in 1905 of a working class family, is a veteran native Communist. * He became a locksmith and a trade union organizer wheh he was only about seventeen. He joined the KPP in the 1920s and was subsequently arrested three times by Polish authorities for his party activities. He served jail terms from 1932 to 1934 and again from 1936 to 1939. Gomułka's whereabouts in the intervening period (1934–36) are still obscure. According to some sources, he studied at the International Lenin School in Moscow; according to others he never left Poland .³ Gomułka did not choose to go from the Nazi to the Russian occupied part of Poland after the outbreak of the War; this decision may well have saved him from liquidation or imprisonment by Stalin's police. His activities and whereabouts between 1939 and 1941, however, are shrouded in obscurity. He may have been active in some of the minuscule, and clandestine, political successors to the Party which developed on a local basis in German-occupied Poland. Almost certainly, this was a period of political hibernation for him, during which his hopes must have been riveted upon a reversal of Soviet foreign policy, a reversal which would once again legitimize Polish communism in Moscow's view, sanction patriotic resistance to the Nazis and, in fact, ressurect the Party as a serious political force in Poland.

Shortly after June 22, 1941, when these hopes were at last realized through the Nazi attack on Russia, Gomułka directed one of the first Moscow-oriented partisan detachments. He was among the founders

---

*When Gomułka was a youngster, his family had emigrated to the United States for a brief period and Gomułka's father at one time worked in a Pennsylvania coal mine.

of the PPR in January 1942 and in November 1943 became Secretary General of the Party following the execution by the Gestapo of his two predecessors, Marceli Nowotko and Paweł Finder. Gomułka remained at this post until the Party purge of September 1948 when he was expelled from all his offices and stripped of his Party membership. He returned as the undisputed leader of Polish Communism, following several years of detention at the hands of his own Party comrades, in the upheaval of October 1956.

In December 1970, in the wake of the rioting and violence occasioned by a drastic price-increase decree, Gomułka resigned as the Party's First Secretary. The official reason was ill health; Gomułka's "indisposition", however, was shared by several of his most prominent associates. Among those ousted from top Party and Government posts were Marian Spychalski, erstwhile Minister of Defense and President of the Council of State; Zenon Kliszko, ideologist and organizational expert; Ignacy Loga-Sowiński, head of Poland's Party-run trade unions, Bolesław Jaszczuk, a co-formulator of Gomułka's economic policy. The new leadership, headed by Edward Gierek, did not strip Gomułka of his Party membership or charge him with criminal or treasonable activities as was customary for fallen leaders in the heyday of Stalinism. But it condemned his methods of rule, assailed his errors and, for all practical purposes, reduced him to the role of a private citizen. Thus ended the longest period of personal leadership in Poland's modern history.

Still another significant type of Communist leader is Józef Cyrankiewicz, Gomułka's second-in-command since 1956, and Poland's Premier from 1954 until 1970. Cyrankiewicz is a co-opted member in the service of the Party. He joined the Communists only after they had succeeded to power. His background is a striking contrast to Gomułka's or Bierut's. Cyrankiewicz was born in 1911, son of middle-class parents; he studied law at the Jagiellonian University at Kraków and from 1933 until 1939 was an active member of the Polish Socialist Party (PPS). He rose to a position of local leadership as the Party's secretary in the Kraków district. During the war he spent several years in the Oświęcim (Auschwitz) and Mauthausen concentration camps where, it has been alleged, he met several Communist prisoners who persuaded him of the desirability of post-war collaboration between the two workers' parties. Since 1945, Cyrankiewicz has been a faithful supporter of the regime and rendered it a crucial service in bringing about the Socialist-Communist (PPS-PPR) merger of 1948. Cyrankiewicz has sat on the PZPR Politburo ever since—until the December 1970 upheaval. Following the departure of Gomułka, Cyrankiewicz shared the role of a scapegoat and was deprived of his posts as Premier and member of the Politburo. In 1971, he was given the relatively figurehead post of President of the Council of State.

The Party's current First Secretary, Edward Gierek, was born in 1913; he represents a relatively new technocratic or managerial type of leadership. He could be better described as a "bureaucrat-technician" than a "revolutionary", an "agitator", or a "conspirator". Like Gomułka, Gierek is a man of impeccably proletarian background. His father, a Silesian miner, emigrated to France in 1923, where Edward grew up and eventually himself worked as a miner in the French coal fields during the 1920s and 1930s. He had joined the French Communist Party at the age of eighteen and participated in several Party-organized strikes. After a brief return to Poland during the 1930s, Gierek went to Belgium, where he headed the Polish section of the Belgian Communist Party and was active in the underground movement during World War II. He returned to Poland only in 1948, joined the newly formed PZPR, and in 1951 became a regional Party secretary in his native Silesia. In that year he also enrolled in a university-level mining school becoming a fully qualified mining engineer in 1954. It was also in 1954 that Gierek became a deputy to the Sejm and a member of the PZPR Central Committee. In 1956 he ascended to the Politburo.

Since the 1950s he had developed a reputation for managerial skill and ability to defend the interests of his particular constituents—the workers and miners of industrial Silesia. Using his leverage in Party councils, Gierek saw to it that the wages, bonuses, and working conditions accorded to his constituents were the best in Poland. Since the rich Silesian region has produced some 90 percent of Poland's coal, 80 percent of its zinc and over 50 percent of the country's steel and electrical energy, Gierek has become known as the "Polish Tschombe." Politically, Gierek has always been a flexible man. In the 1950s, he could be described as a Gomułka "liberal". In the late 1960s Gierek had managed to remain at once the supporter of an ultra-nationalist, authoritarian, and anti-semitic Party opposition to Gomułka, and simultaneously a beacon of hope and "thaw" for the Polish consumer. Unlike his predecessor, Gierek had always evinced concern for the provision of basic amenities to the people. Indeed, Gomułka personally represented an austere style of Communist puritanism, living as he did in a modest three-room Warsaw apartment. Gierek, who has aspired to reward Polish workers with low-priced automobiles has been known to use no less than three himself—a Mercedes, a Citroen, and a Soviet Tschaika—in addition to a small airplane. The economic crisis of December 1970 brought Edward Gierek to party leadership as the man most likely to win the nation's confidence on bread-and-butter issues. In the midst of the economic and political crisis of 1970–71, Gierek has reverted to a moderate liberal stance, emphasizing the fulfillment of consumer wants, responding to mass grievances and the democratization of the processes of government.

The organization of the Polish Party closely resembles the Soviet and the prevalently East European model. The Party's primary organization network combines the economic and territorial principles. Party groups are organized in shops, factories, public agencies, the armed forces, and places of employment. These "work groups" are integrated in a four-level territorial scheme: precinct, county or town, provincial, and finally nation-wide organizations. Nominally, the Polish party operates under the "Leninist norms of democratic centralism." All officials are subject to election and party resolutions and policy decisions are subject to majority approval at each appropriate level of party organization. The leadership at each party level is required to submit reports to membership meetings and the latter are open to discussion by all the party members. On the other hand, decisions of higher party bodies (e.g., the provincial organization *vis à vis* the precinct party) are unconditionally binding upon the lower party bodies. Within each level, the minority on any issue is similarly required to unreservedly support the decision of the majority. The rules of party discipline preclude the creation of any groupings to promote or oppose policies or persons in the interval between party meetings and elections.

The apex of authority is statutorily lodged in the Central Committee, the Party's highest elected, deliberative organ. The Central Committee is elected by a Party Congress made up of delegates chosen by the country's provincial party organizations. Rank-and-file Party members can never exercise direct choices in the selection of this important body. Their participation is confined to voting for delegates to the communal organizations; these in turn choose the provincial delegates and the latter the National Party Congress. At each level of organization, executive responsibility is delegated to a committee and a secretariat who, between plenary meetings, exercise full powers of their particular Party units.

In practice, this system consolidates power in the hands of the Party executives and subordinates the rank-and-file to the central leadership. Party secretaries dominate the processes of election, discussion, and policy formulation. They control nominations for all Party offices and the nominations are almost always tantamount to elections. They

exercise preponderant influence in determing the timetable and scope
of Party programs. They are the fulltime manipulators of the know-
how, the manpower, and the material resources of the Party. This
inner Party bureaucracy constitutes the "eyes and ears" of the national
Party leadership, keeping close watch over the personnel and deport-
ment of Party units. It transmits policy directives from the "top" and
the responses and pressures from "below." The bureaucracy's power
in terms of patronage, in terms of influence on administrative decisions, and also in terms of shaping public policy, is firmly anchored in
its loyalty and responsiveness to the central Party authorities. Of the
approximately 2.0 million party members and candidates in 1968 some
10 percent constituted the full-time cadre of Party bureaucracy.

Since 1945 the Communists have held six national congresses (four
as the PZPR): in 1945, 1948, 1954, 1959, 1964, 1968 and 1971. The
1945 meeting was prior to the merger with the Socialists. The number
of delegates at these meetings has averaged about 1400. Data from
some of the congresses indicate that the overwhelming majority of the
participants are persons whose full time occupations are as Party and
Government administrators. In 1959, the Party bureaucrats alone accounted for more than 40 percent or 587 out of the 1431 delegates.

The policy-making organ elected by each national congress—the
Central Committee—has varied in size from forty-seven members and
candidate-members in 1945 to 139 in 1962. The number of members
was first significantly increased after the PPR-PPS merger. Forty-four
former socialists including Jozef Cyrankiewicz were elected to the
PZPR Central Committee but were outnumbered there two to one by
former PPR men. The composition of the Central Committee has
traditionally accorded the heaviest over-representation to the Party's
professionals. In 1962, full-time Party workers accounted for 47.9
percent of the Committee (67 out of 139) despite the fact that they
represented only abut 10 percent of the total party membership. The
second largest component in 1962 was the Government bureaucracy:
ministers, secretaries, directors, and sundry officials, 32.9 percent or
forty-five out of 139. This group was actually the largest single component in the Central Committee in 1949 and 1955—barely ahead of the
Party workers. As a professional category, the Government bureaucrats have undoubtedly always accounted for a substantial majority of
occupations within the post-war Polish Communist movement. Mass
organizations, representing trade unions, youth cooperative, cultural
and women's groups, have generally represented upwards of ten percent of the membership; the military and the police upwards of five.

The key executive organs of the Central Committee are the Politburo and the Secretariat which, between them, effectively control the policies and operations of both Party and State in Poland. Both of these organs are statutorily accountable to the Central Committee and receive their mandate from it. In practice, and strikingly so before 1956, the Politburo and the Secretariat have often acted with only perfunctory reference to the Central Committee. The latter was seldom convoked before 1956 in violation of the Party's own rules.

Just as in the Soviet case, the Polish Politburo's work and its procedures are shrouded in secrecy. It is generally believed to operate not merely as one policy-making group but also through smaller, specialized subcommittees and *ad hoc* teams dealing with specific problems and accountable to the Politburo as a whole.

The criticisms levelled at Gomułka by his successors confirm the impression that at least since the mid-1960s the PZPR had substantially reverted to the secretive and arbitrary processes of policy-making typical of Stalinism. In 1971, Gierek vowed to infuse new methods, emphasizing openness, congeniality, and dialogue, as the chief means of reinvigorating the Party and increasing its influence in the society.

In 1970, just prior to the December upheaval, the Politburo consisted of thirteen full members: Władysław Gomułka, Jozef Cyrankiewicz, Marian Spychalski, Ignacy Loga-Sowinski, Zenon Kliszko, Bolesław Jaszczuk, Ryszard Strzelecki, Edward Gierek, Stefan Jędrychowski, Wojciech Jaruzelski, Stanisław Kociołek, Władysław Kruczek, and Jozef Tejchma. There were four candidate members, without voting rights: General Mieczysław Moczar, Mieczysław Jagielski, Piotr Jaroszewicz, and Jan Szydlak.*

The Secretariat, headed by Gomułka, was made up of nine principal members or secretaries. Seven of these nine (Gomułka, Kliszko, Jaszczuk, Strzelecki, Tejchma, Moczar, and Szydlak) were concurrently members, or candidate members, of the Poliburo.

The Secretariat is officially charged with the mission of control over the implementation of Party policy and the selection of Party personnel. Its work is actually subdivided in more than thirty bureaus, departments, and special commissions which cover different areas of concern to the party. Illustrative of their great variety are the Institute of Social Science, until 1967 directed by the "revisionist" (and thence purged) party ideologist, Adam Schaff; a Press Bureau; Departments of

---

*Following the election of Gierek as First Secretary, Moczar and Jaroszewicz were elevated to full membership while the first seven members, i.e., Gomułka and his staunchest allies, were eased out in "several installments".

Agriculture and Foreign Affairs; a Central Party Group to Combat Corruption; and Commissions on such matters as Sports and Tourism, Youth, Education, Publishing, and Light Industry.

Just as within the PZPR the top leadership controls all of the principal directing organs through overlapping membership, so analogously is this control projected outward. The principal leaders of the Government (Council of Ministers) and of the Legislature (Council of State) are also members of the PZPR Politburo and members of the PZPR Secretariat and Central Committee.

Much the same is the case with the principal mass organizations, above all the trade unions. These latter groups serve, as in the Soviet Union, as transmission belts and links for the implementation of Party policies throughout the country. Among them are such organizations as the League of Women; the All-Polish Peace Committee; the League of Soldiers' Friends; the Society of Children's Friends; the Union of Socialist and Rural Youth and the Union of Fighters for Freedom and Democracy. All of these are organizations which include Communist and non-Communist members but which the Party regards as instruments of its policy and in which it plays an open and dominant part.

Twenty-two Polish trade unions, covering the most diverse occupations ranging from chemists and radio announcers to agricultural workers and miners, are united in the so-called Central Council of Trade Unions. Its total membership was 8.5 million persons in 1968, including some 3 million women, more than 90 percent of Polish employees. The Council was led by Politburo member, Ignacy Loga-Sowiński.* The Polish Unions participate in the administration of welfare funds and worker rest homes, mediation of labor disputes, and the representational functions of the Conferences of Worker-Self-Government. In the 1950s, they were instrumental in enabling the Bierut regime to evade nearly every provision of the regime's labor legislation to force the pace of industrial production. Acting as agents of the Party and controllers of the labor force rather than representatives of the workers, the Union leaders supported indeterminate "suspension" of legislative safeguards with respect to hours, conditions of work, labor discipline, wage agreements, age and health standards of employees, and the like. In this sense, the malfunction of the unions, their failure to represent workers claims and grievances to the regime, was one of

---

*The January 1971 replacement of Loga-Sowiński by an old Stalinist, Władysław Kruczek, cast doubt among Polish workers as to Gierek's seriousness with respect to democratizing Polish trade unions.

the underlying causes of the grave labor unrest in Poland in 1970 and 1971.

Another group of organizations, representing a more indirect affiliation with the Party, is exemplified by such groups as the so-called Patriot Priests and the Catholic *Pax* movement, both organized in the 1940s and aimed at the penetration of Catholic opinion. Cooperation between the Party and groups of this sort is based on shared attitudes, or interests, and upon indirect manipulation (such as provision of material incentives to the leadership) rather than on overt PZPR Party member participation.

Among affiliates of this character are the PZPR's two adjunct parties: The United Peasant Party (Zjednoczone Stronnictwo Ludowe or Z.S.L.) and the Democratic Party (Stronnictwo Demokratyczne or S.D.). Both of these parties are formally pledged to assist the PZPR in achieving the Communists' objectives, though in different social sectors: the Z.S.L. among the peasants and the S.D. among the urban middle class and intelligentsia.

The Z.S.L. originated as the Peasant Party (Stronnictwo Ludowe—S.L.) made up almost entirely of Communists and obscure fellow travellers. In 1947, following the destruction of Mikołajczyk's genuine mass party, the PSL (Polskie Stronnictwo Ludowe—Polish Peasant Party) the Communists promoted a "merger" of their bogus group with those remnants of the Mikołajczyk party which were willing to go along with them. Thus came into being the Z.S.L. in 1949. It has been a partner of the PZPR in the Front of National Unity in all elections since 1952. In 1969 party membership was about 380,000. Its organization has been strictly territorial, ascending from village, commune, and county to province and national levels. It has attempted to organize support for Communist policies in the countryside, where the appeal and followings of the PZPR have been particularly anemic. From the standpoint of pluralistic tendencies, it is the ZSL rank and file, rather than the leadership, which is worthy of notice. The ZSL at grass roots levels includes some "undigested," strongly anti-communist elements. Its potential for opposition at the local level is probably considerable. In 1956–57, the rank-and-file apparently demanded opposition, not cooperation with the PZPR, and large-scale purges of local party bureaucracy became necessary to keep the ZSL in line. Only with this considerable prodding has the United Peasant Party returned to its expected outward docility of the early 1950s as a participant in "the construction of socialism by workers and peasants," and in the fulfilment of current economic plans set by the PZPR.

Z.S.L. has been led by Czesław Wycech, who has also served as

Speaker (Marshal) of the Sejm.* Among the Party's principal leaders have been Bolesław Podedworny, Józef Ozga-Michalski and Franciszek Gesing.

The smaller adjunct of the PZPR is the Democratic Party of about 85,000 members drawn from the professional strata, white collar workers, and a sprinkling of small proprietors and artisans. The Democratic Party traces its lineage to a group founded in 1938 by certain liberal Polish intellectuals, but the Party grew to considerable size only after the Communist seizure of power. Like the ZSL, the SD has officially defined its tasks and programs in terms of an alliance with the proletariat, led by the PZPR, and the struggle for the realization of socialism and communism in Poland.

The Democrats are led by Zygmunt Moskwa as Chairman; Stanisław Kulczyński, Jan Karol Wende, and Włodzimierz Lechowicz, are the principal leaders behind him. The party's distinctiveness has been its relatively positive attitude to private enterprise, which it has occasionally defended as still "useful" and "effective" in the transitional phase of socialist construction toward the truly classless society. Because of this stand, the SD has been organizing within its ranks strata with a maximum interest in prolonging the "transition" and delaying the "arrival" of the classless utopia. Again, as in the case of the ZSL, the link between the character of the rank-and-file membership and the SD leadership has been relatively tenuous and artificial.

From the very beginning of their rule the Communists themselves have been plagued with internal as well as external difficulties. Not only has the Party always met with serious opposition among the people at large, but it has never been able to shape its own followers into a reasonable facsimile of a monolith. Partly this has been a problem of size. The Party, as the original PPR, claimed only 4000 members in 1942, and only 20,000 in 1944. Just before the merger with the Socialists in 1948 the PPR stood at the one million membership mark. This was immediately increased by a further one-half million as a result of the merger. Following several purges, the Party's membership has levelled off at about 1.3 million in the late 1950s and increased to over 1.6 million in the 1960s. It reached 2.0 million in 1968. This great and rapid expansion of membership has diluted the original core of the Party with elements of doubtful Communist identification. As Professor M. K. Dziewanowski put it in 1959:[5]

"... despite the lip service constantly paid to Marxian, proletarian internationalism and the 'Soviet-Polish brotherhood' by the party rank and file, the

---

*Wycech was replaced by Stanisław Gucwa in February 1971.

party at the bottom became more and more permeated with 'petty bourgeois, nationalistic,' and even religious sentiments common to broad masses of the Polish people. Most party members had vivid memories of the Stalinist purges, the liquidation of the CPP, and the deportations of the years 1939–1941. They had witnessed the behavior of the 'liberating' Soviet troops in Poland, their looting and raping; they knew about the . . . Katyn massacre, the role played by the Soviet army during the Warsaw uprising, etc."

In trying to become a reasonably popular political force in a nation singularly hostile to their own outlook and traditions, the Communists have confronted a dilemma which they have not been able to solve. Their attempt to absorb within the party much of the administrative and technological apparatus of the Polish state rendered them prone to political-ideological erosion. Conversely, by assigning themselves a virtual monopoly of power in the state, the Communists became a natural objective of all those seeking to share in the spoils and perquisites of power and also of those anxious to influence the course of public affairs even if privately opposed to the Party's rule and its tenets. To some extent, the problem in Poland has been analogous to that in the other states of Eastern Europe and even to the Soviets'.

The larger the Party has grown, the less proletarian it has tended to become, both in terms of the social origin and the occupational structure of its membership. As Richard F. Staar has pointed out, the percentage of industrial workers in the PZPR has steadily declined between 1949 and 1961 while actually the total number of workers and their share in the Polish labor force has been greatly increased in the same period. Where in 1949 20.4 percent of industrial workers were PZPR members, only 6.3 percent belonged in 1961. The largest group in the party became white collar workers—mainly administrators and officials. Where the party has been successful in recruiting the administrators of Government and industry, it has lagged in the recruitment of workers, students, persons under the age of twenty-five, and women. It has also done very poorly among the peasantry, still a formidable force in Poland. In 1961 the Party claimed only 15 percent of its members as being either peasant or of farm-worker backgrounds.

Party policy in Poland has gone through at least seven major, distinctive phases. These are (1) the united front "democratic" period until 1948; (2) the Stalinist period from 1948 until early 1954; (3) the mild liberalization from 1954 until the October 1956 revolution; (4) the establishment of Poland's relative autonomy within the Soviet sphere of influence and the more serious changes of 1956–57; (5) the stabilization of Communist rule, a return to "recompression" less harsh than the Stalinist regime but more stringent than had been

widely hoped and anticipated in 1956–57; (6) since 1967 a period
combining popular unrest with increasing repression by, and crisis
within, the Party, threatening Gomułka's leadership; (7) the second
revolution of December 1970, and its aftermath.

Until 1948 Party policy still reflected the tactics employed in the
seizure of power. As summarized in Chapter I, the PPR stood for land
reform—by which it did *not* mean collectivization but a redistribution
of land holdings without compensation to those expropriated. It championed a policy of alliance and friendship with the USSR, and the
desirability of Poland's ties to the West as well. Having acquiesced in
the Soviet annexation of Lwów and Wilno, the PPR supported Stalin's
view that Poland should be territorially compensated at the expense
of Germany and championed the Oder-Neisse line as Poland's just and
immutable frontier. The Communists also pledged themselves to the
nationalization of major economic enterprises in industry, mining,
transportation, utilities, and finance. They did not threaten the smaller
entrepreneurs. Even the Communists' constitutional principles were
in this early phase of their rule "purer than pure." Poland before 1939
operated under two constitutions: a parliamentary one of 1921, mod-
eled on the French Third Republic and an authoritarian, "presidential" constitution since 1935. The Polish Government-in-Exile always
maintained the validity of the latter, and claimed to derive its legitimate powers from its dispensations. The Communists made themselves the defenders of the more liberal, parliamentary system and
indeed until 1952 professed to rely on the 1921 Constitution, albeit
with "modifications" such as the abolition of the Senate and other
temporary adaptations of their so-called Small Constitution of 1947.[6]
If despite its program the Party's popularity in those days was not
greater, this was due to the suspicion and resentment engendered by
the PPR's Russian backing, the profound mistrust of its future inten-
tions, and its *de facto* treatment of opposition.

During this period the PPR registered a mass influx of new membership; there were no substantial purges or strong-arm methods directed
within, that is at the Party itself. Power in the PPR was still significantly
balanced between such trusted Muscovites as Bierut, Berman, and
their Soviet aides, on the one hand, and a native group led by the First
Secretary, Gomułka, and including Spychalski, Kliszko, Loga-Sowinski, and others.

Outwardly, the Party's rule was characterized by considerable physical violence. All sorts of enemies and suspected-enemies, people who
were identified with the London exiles, or the Home Army (A.K.) were
being arrested, imprisoned, and liquidated. The Party was fighting a

small-scale civil war in some areas of Poland against the surviving elements of the right-wing nationalist underground—the NSZ (Narodowe Siły Zbrojne—National Armed Forces). It suffered considerable casualties in the process of this "pacification."

In April of 1947, Gomułka wrote in the official Party organ, *Nowe Drogi*, that Poland would pursue her own path of social development, without the need of a one party dictatorship on the Soviet pattern. This position ran counter to Stalin's policy of rendering the East European nations miniature copies of the Soviet Union, wholly subservient to Russian leadership and example.

Gomułka's ideas of the 1942–1947 period had made him an ideal Communist leader in a period when both the Soviet Union and the Party were trying to present a broadly attractive "united front" image, alike in Poland and internationally.[7] Gomułka stood for cooperation with other political parties. By his own later admission, he had even considered at one time cooperation with General Sikorski's London Government. Gomułka opposed reforms carried out at the point of a gun—specifically, forced collectivization following the Soviet model. Obviously he was the man most likely to allay the fears of the peasants. He was an earnest advocate of Polish-Soviet collaboration but insisted on the complete autonomy and equality of the Poles in managing their own affairs. To regard Russia as an enemy was, for Gomułka, a tragic mistake, even a crime. But for Polish Communists to behave in Poland as if they were in Russia was equally a mistake.

When the initial seizure of power in Poland was completed, however, and the breach with the West became all but complete, Gomułka had lost his usefulness so far as the Kremlin was concerned. Moreover, like Tito, he became an obvious stumbling block to the further "sovietization" of Poland. His ideas, understandably, led to his removal as First Secretary of the Party. Moscow repeatedly demanded his public trial and execution, a fate from which the misgivings and possibly latent loyalties of his Polish Party colleagues saved him. In any event, Gomułka, accused of "Titoism" and "bourgeois nationalism," was removed from all his Party offices and expelled from the PZPR in December 1948. From 1951 until the end of 1954 Gomułka was imprisoned, a fate shared by most of his erstwhile political associates.

Unlike similar "bourgeois nationalist deviationists" in Czechoslovakia (Slansky) or Hungary (Rajk), the Polish Communists were not executed nor were they even put on trial. Their lives were spared and this "leniency" displayed toward them by the regime was symbolic of other, wider issues. Even at the height of Stalin's "sovietization" of Eastern Europe, Poland remained something of a laggard. She succumbed to less agricultural collectivization and undoubtedly enjoyed more religious and personal freedom than any other Soviet satellite of the 1948–1956 period.

Even so, Poland went through a period of fearful repression and regimentation. Party policy after 1948 was a dreary echo of Soviet ideology and propaganda. The Soviet Union and its glorious leader, Stalin, could do no wrong. The Party's security apparatus was in its heyday. To depart or challenge Party orthodoxy in any matter, cultural or intellectual, let alone political or economic, was to risk arrest, torture, and even execution. The security police became the chief enforcer of party policy and orthodoxy. People disappeared from the streets or in the dead of night, often never to be heard from again.[8]

It appears that during this period much of the job of governing Poland was done at the explicit instructions of the Soviet Union, communicated either directly from the Kremlin or through the Soviet Ambassador in Warsaw to Bierut, Berman, and others. And it is beyond any doubt that many of the key officials carrying out policy decisions were Soviet Russian personnel, headed by the erstwhile Red Army Marshal, K. Rokossovsky (USSR's recently deceased Vice-Minister of Defense). During this period Poland was akin to a colonial domain of the USSR.

Stalin's death brought about the beginnings of a "thaw." The all-wise and all-powerful leader was gone, and Soviet leadership under Malenkov was still new, insecure, and divided in a struggle for power among Beria, Khrushchev, and the Malenkov-Molotov group. It attempted to establish itself by a policy of concessions and relaxation both at home and abroad. Terrorism, extreme deprivation of the consumer in favor of armament and heavy industry, international tensions —all these were significantly relieved. The grim Lavrenti Beria was dispatched. The impact of the changes on Poland was all but unavoidable.

In faithfully following the Soviet example, the Polish Party was bound to make analogous shifts of policy and open some doors which, once opened, might never be closed again. The culmination of this process was the Twentieth Congress of the Soviet Communist Party early in 1956, in which Khrushchev exposed all of Stalin's rule to a withering critique. In the face of all these developments the Polish Party could hardly react fast enough.

The moderate changes promoted by Edward Ochab who had succeeded Bierut as PZPR leader in April 1956 seemed generally inadequate. A ferment of publicly voiced doubts, self-accusations, and confessions began to pour forth from the Communists themselves. To a great extent it was the Party's own intellectuals, writers, and poets like Leon Pasternak and Adam Ważyk who paved the way for a major upheaval. Jakub Berman and other sinister figures in the police apparatus were dismissed from office. But all this was hardly enough in the face of mounting grass-roots demands for a thorough break with the Stalinist past in all respects—economically, culturally, and politically.

Pent-up dissatisfaction among the people with the economic austerity, the drabness and coercion of communist rule manifested itself violently on June 28, 1956 in Poznań. At least fifty persons were killed, hundreds wounded in street demonstrations. Worker disaffection was deep and spreading. It seemed as if the regime would momentarily become the target of popular revolution. With the tide of public opinion running so heavily against it, many people in Poland and elsewhere believed that only the Red Army's intervention could save the Party's rule in Poland. The events of "Black Thursday" in Poznań were not only a strong demonstration of popular opinion against the regime; they also indicated the disturbing unreliability and ineffectiveness of the Party's own apparatus, of the armed forces and of the police.[9]

Against the background of Poznań, the Party leadership under Edward Ochab convoked the VII Plenum (plenary meeting) of the Central Committee—in July in Warsaw. The Party meeting was a public confirmation of the economic failures of the regime. It exposed the extent to which the Party had sacrificed the material welfare of the Polish people to the tasks of industrialization. It also produced a clash on a future course of remedies and reforms between a neo-Stalinist 'conservative' wing led by Zenon Nowak, Franciszek Mazur, Jóźwiak-Witold, and Marshal Rokossovsky and a 'liberal' group led by Ochab, Cyrankiewicz, Rapacki, and Gierek.

The conservatives, having met at a castle in nearby Natolin prior to the Plenum, were henceforth dubbed as the "Natolin Group." Two other members of the Politburo, Alexander Zawadzki and Roman Zambrowski, were as yet publicly uncommitted. Both groups sought to bring Gomułka back into the Party as a means of shoring up its threadbare public image. The liberals, however, wanted to vest Gomułka with full power as the only possible savior of Polish Communism. The Natolin group wanted him only as a kind of "liberal window dressing."

The Natolin group was widely reported to be seeking armed Soviet assistance, if necessary, to prevent any far-reaching changes from taking place. The issue within the Party was largely formulated in terms of Poland's relationship to the Soviet Union. The Natolin conservatives believed a return of Gomułka and any further democratization or liberalization of the regime would lead to a breach with the Soviet Union—one which they hoped the Soviet Union would not tolerate and the "liberals" would not ultimately want to risk. They feared, as apparently Khrushchev himself did at the time, that Gomułka's return might spell the end of Communist rule in Poland.

A strange atmosphere of incipient revolution and patriotic war against Soviet domination swept Poland in October 1956. A Soviet delegation composed of Khrushchev, Kaganovich, Mikoyan, and Molotov came to Warsaw to warn the Polish "liberals" against any "anti-Soviet" coup on their part. They clearly wondered whether Gomułka's incipient return to power would be a prelude to an attempted "decommunization" of Poland and her withdrawal from the Warsaw Pact. There were rumors of Soviet troops massing on Polish frontiers; the tragedy of Hungary was just beginning to unfold. But the Polish Central Committee stood its ground. Gomułka was elected the PZPR's First Secretary. Ironically, in 1956, he, who in 1945 was regarded by most Poles as a Soviet agent, was now a national hero as a symbol of Polish resistance to Soviet domination. Rokossovsky and various other Russian experts and advisers were sent home.

Gomułka's program of 1956 was a far reaching indictment of the Stalinist past.[10] He renounced compulsory collectivization, demanded democratization of party and government institutions and worker participation in management; he demanded more freedom to experiement with and discuss new ideas.* He reaffirmed Poland's right to its own individual "road to socialism," and emphasized co-equality with the Soviet Communist Party in Place of subservience.

What Gomułka did not do, and this was in many ways even more important, was to threaten the basic framework of Soviet-Polish alliance as embodied in the Warsaw Pact. Nor did he suggest a transition from the essentially one-party Communist rule to a genuinely democratic multi-party system. Polish Communism was to be improved, purified, and democratized, not abolished. Gomułka's commitment to such a relatively moderate program made his regime safe from the brutal intervention of Soviet military power that fell upon Hungary within a few days of the 'Eighth Plenum.'

On the other hand, this basic commitment to change *within* rather than *against* the hitherto existent communist system rendered Gomułka's rule in Poland since 1957 a disappointment to most of his compatriots. His regime was caught in the vise of competing demands

*In domestic affairs, Gomułka's early "liberalism" clearly paralleled Gierek's 1970–1971 stance.

for the maintenance of some form of Party orthodoxy and effective monopoly of Party power on the one hand, and the expectations and the hopes of a nationalistic and individualistic people on the other.

In domestic politics, Gomułka supported the ideal of realizing Communism in a way which would take account of specifically Polish conditions, and one which could be made somewhat more genuinely acceptable to a large segment of the Polish people. In foreign affairs, the cornerstone of his position continued to be a close alliance with the USSR because of the German threat in the west and also as an indirect support to the maintenance of the Communist system in Poland.

Within these parameters of orthodoxy, Gomułka managed to disappoint most Poles, reassure the Russians, and taper off the processes of reform in Poland at a point far short of a genuinely open society. In his November 1956 visit to Moscow Gomułka acknowledged "the leading role" of the USSR in the world Communist movement but insisted that Poland had a right to follow its own path of social development. He publicly asserted that Communism would succeed in Poland only if she enjoyed full equality with all other Communist states and only if the Polish Party were allowed to adapt itself to the specifically Polish circumstances in which it worked. This turned out to be the last occasion on which Gomułka parted with Soviet leaders on a note of public defiance or implicit threat. His message apparently was at last understood and accepted in Moscow.

Among the changes which Gomułka's regime brought about in 1956–57, probably the most striking to Poles and foreigners alike was a new freedom from fear. With drastic curbs imposed upon the political police, and with the relaxation of censorship, people began to feel less constraint in speech and action in communication with one another than undoubtedly at any time since 1939. Gomułka also moved to democratize Polish political life by allowing more meaningful participation to people through such measures as the new electoral laws, the Workers' Councils, and the opening up of discussion within the Party itself. For the first time in a decade, Poland became open to visitors from the West, and the West itself became accessible to thousands of Poles through tourism and through cultural exchange programs. Gomułka's regime broke down Poland's international isolation of the Stalinist era. In this particular respect, his reforms have proved enduring as the volume of East-West travel has grown steadily since 1956. In economics, Gomułka adopted a more conciliatory and encouraging posture toward the peasant and the private enterpreneur; he lifted the threat of forced collectivization from the land; relaxed the harsh, punitive methods of labor discipline; by revising the state's investment policies he somewhat redressed the lot of the consumer, with the promise, or at least the widespread hope, of further improvements.

Perhaps the greatest and most fateful accomplishment of the 1956–57 period was the unprecedented disclosure of past wrongs which the Party had inflicted on the country. This in itself gave rise to expectations that somehow forthcoming remedies would be in proportion to the magnitude of past evils. But in opting for a course of moderate, cautious, restrained reforms, both politically and economically, Gomułka failed to breathe new life into the Polish Communist party, and harness the wave of popular enthusiasm which had swept Poland in October 1956. He did not offer the Party clear-cut direction. His policies had been eclectic, balancing various factions, moderating pressures from the extremes, and alternating restrictions with relaxations of controls in various areas of Polish life. Over the course of years since 1956, Gomułka gradually retreated, albeit not always consistently, from the "liberalism" of the Polish October, and established a personal image of aloofness and conservatism, of an inherent suspicion of far-reaching change.

One year after the revolution to which the writers had made such a significant contribution, Gomułka demanded a reimposition of censorship from the official, Party-controlled Writers' Union. His request was grudgingly supported by most members; some, however, resigned in protest both from the Union and from the Party. Among these was Adam Ważyk whose "Poem for Adults" was one of the prime stimulants and intellectual symbols of the Revolution. Gomułka failed to disassociate his regime from the unsavory influences of Bolesław Piasecki's *Pax,* even though the latter had been denounced both by Cardinal Wyszyński and the more liberal elements within the Party itself as an odious synthesis of Stalinism, pre-war fascism, and rabid anti-semitism. In April 1958 Gomułka publicly reasserted that Polish labor could not expect to enjoy the right to strike under socialism. Presumably no repetitions of Poznań were to be allowed. In his lengthy report to the Party's Central Committee in October 1959, Gomułka reserved his sharpest attack for the "revisionists," not for those "dogmatists" who presumably shouldered the real responsibility for the evils of pre-1956 days.

"Revisionism" has been one of the major and recurrent problems for the PZPR since 1956–57. The term itself in the context of Polish politics has covered a multitude of Communist sins, most of them revolving around a repudiation of the Party's leading role—i.e., a willingness to share power with non-Marxist and anti-Marxist parties under some form of open, competitive political system—or even conduct which, indirectly, would tend to bring this about. From time to time, spokesmen within the ruling Party have defined, interpreted, or "reinterpreted" the Marxian doctrine in such a way as to invalidate or at least seriously undermine virtually all of the hitherto sacred verities of official Soviet and Polish Communism. Their policy proposals, demands, or conclusions have included abandonment of one-party dictatorship; freedom for political opposition; complete independence from Soviet Russia; restoration of an essentially private enterprise economic system; an end to the promotion of world-wide revolutionary activities by Communists; full-fledged collaboration with non-Communist states; an end to every form of censorship and political-cultural regimentation and many others.[11]

Illustrative of revisionist tendencies have been the professional associations affiliated with the Party, above all perhaps the Writers Union. In 1956 its members helped prepare the intellectual and emotional climate of the October revolution. The Union was instrumental in bringing about the downfall of one of Poland's chief Stalinist leaders, Jakub Berman, when the latter attempted to chastise the writers for their failings in an August 1955 Warsaw meeting. Venting long accummulated grievances, the Union gave Berman a crushing public rebuff which led directly to his resignation as Vice-Premier. Similarly, the intellectuals' club *Krzywe Koło* (Crooked Circle), which subjected various aspects of past Communist policy to scathing criticism and sharp debate by a variety of more or less revisionist ideologues, also played a role in preparing the ground for the 1956 changes.

Individuals and groups such as these have continued to play a similar role, if less spectacularly; that is, they have represented and articulated different viewpoints, interests, and orientations within the Party itself. An important example of the revisionist potential within the highest councils of the PZPR was furnished by no less a figure than Adam Schaff, the Party's principal ideologist in the mid-1960s. Schaff's 1965 book, *Marxism and the Individual* (Marksizm i Jednostka ludzka) raised some fundamental doubts about the Party's doctrine, with all the implications about its omniscience and its role in society.[12]

Looking at Marxism from the vantage point of the individual, Schaff came to the pessimistic conclusion that the problem of man's alienation from society and from his environment* is not really solved by the

---

*"alienation," as used by Schaff is a broad term covering the sum of socially created evil and oppression to which man is subject.

establishment of socialist relations of production, according to the Marxian sequence of revolution and social development. On the contrary, the gist of Schaff's argument was that the "expropriation of the expropriators," the control of the means of production and distribution by a worker peasant state, and the planned expansion of productive forces under its auspices, created new, additional problems for man. Schaff openly discussed the evils and threats posed by the stifling bureaucratization of life under communism; dictatorship, violence, and the emergence of new privileged elites; the suppression of individual and social initiative and creativity in science, art, and culture. He also specifically indicted the Polish party for a hypocritical attitude on human freedom and equality. Where the issue was a remote one and concerned others—Black freedom in South Africa or the United States, for example—the Party would thunder its indignation at the persecutors. Simultaneously, however, Schaff pointed out that it condoned and was insensitive to anti-Semitism within Poland and above all within the ranks of the Party itself. Much of what Schaff wrote was familiar ground to westerners who had read Milovan Djilas or Czesław Miłosz. But coming from a source so officially unimpeachable—a member of the Party's Central Committee and longtime head of its ideological section—it was major news.[13]

Another very important figure among Marxian dissenters has been Leszek Kolakowski, since 1970 an emigré professor of philosophy at Oxford. Author of *Marxism and Beyond* in 1969 and of various other works, Kolakowski used Marxian ideas as points of departure for far-ranging and eclectic social theorizing. His writings challenged and negated some basic postulates of Marxism, particularly historical materialism. By emphasis on the individual, and on the spiritual and moral freedom of man, Kolakowski threatened the Party bureaucracy's vested interest—the maintenance of the propositions that Marxism is TRUTH and that the Party is always right.

If Marxian revisionism were allowed to proliferate, "Communism" would soon cease to be the dogmatic "holy writ" of the Party and become something of a background theme, a loosely articulated ideological "point of departure," no more specific in content or binding upon all political actors than, say, the prevalent norms of liberal democracy in Britain and America. This kind of ideological erosion— or perhaps "proliferation of communism"—would be virtually certain to direct Polish politics to an ever increasing pluralism and openness. If the Party is not always right, if it does not have a claim to a special kind of excellence, why acquiesce in its absolute rule?

In his position of leadership Gomułka was buffeted by pressures both from "below" and "above." The demands for more freedom from the Polish people at large and some segments of the Party have been countered by the demands for the reinforcement of controls by the Party apparatus. In the 1960s Gomułka increasingly responded to these "conservative" pressures from within the Party bureaucracy.

In the 1950s it had been the former Stalinists who, backed by Moscow, fought for the maintenance of the Party's unquestioned supremacy. The original Stalinists, however, had been weakened and discredited. Their leaders, Bierut, Minc, and Berman, have largely succumbed to old age, illness, death, and retirement. Some, like Marshal Rokossovsky, have simply been repatriated to the Soviet Union. Their exposure for complicity in the crimes of the Stalin period has been thorough and damaging. Above all, their reputation for subservience to the Russians is an element of weakness among Poles. The Soviet outlook has also changed since 1953.

The principal opposition to "revisionism" in recent years has come not from the Stalinists of the Natolin group but from the so-called Partisans, led by the Security Police chief General Mieczysław Moczar. On the eve of the Party's Fifth Congress in 1968, it was Moczar who was openly, and to all appearances successfully, challenging Gomułka's leadership. The issues of subversion and the need to purge the Party were the main themes of Moczar's attack.

His "conservatism" has a different political orientation from Stalinism in support of its toughness, though with some common denominators. It is essentially nationalistic, parochial, and outwardly "patriotic." It relies upon an amalgam of ideas drawn as much from Roman Dmowski as from Karl Marx. Authoritarianism, anti-semitism, and the identification of the Polish national interest with a Russian alliance aimed against Germany are its most characteristic features.

Moczar, born in 1913, began his political career as a Communist guerrilla during World War II. He became Head of the Security Police in 1945 and continued in this post until 1956. In the aftermath of the Polish October, Moczar was temporarily demoted to a much less significant post as Minister of State Farms. But he managed to avoid the more serious reprisals meted out to Berman, Radkiewicz, and others in the security apparatus who had been involved in the police persecutions of Stalinism. In fact, within the year, Moczar was back at his job, with the additional title of Vice-Minister of Interior. In 1964 he became Minister of Interior and also Chairman of a powerful veterans' organization "Zbowid"—Związek Bojowników o Wolność i Demokrację, (The Association of Fighters for Freedom and Democracy). Through this group, Moczar has been able to distribute significant patronage to some quarter-million members, thus cultivating a sizeable political clientele. A decoration conferred by Moczar's organization could mean a higher retirement pension, a Government license for running a private store, priority in getting housing, a job, or preference in gaining entry into the school system. Moczar's hold on the police-security apparatus was strengthened by the promotion of his supporters, Szlachcic, to Vice-Minister of Interior in 1962, and General Pietrzak as head of the People's Militia in 1965.

Moczar had also established far-flung connections in the Polish communications media: television, radio, and the press. He had recruited and courted a wide range of allies, including the ex-fascist Bolesław Piasecki, and the ex-Stalinist Politburo leader, Ryszard Strzelecki. In consequence, he has been accused of reversing a famed Leninist motto —to the effect that "those who are not against us are with us."

Appealing to ultra nationalists and ex-Stalinists, Moczar had in fact given these disparate elements a desirable common platform: the maintenance of monolithic central power in the hands of the Party bureaucracy. Moczar hoped that those with a vested interest in the continuance of such power in Poland, and those opposed to a really open society, for whatever reasons (including the Russians), would coalesce behind him. To what positive uses power might be put under Moczar's leadership, however, is not at all clear. He has given no indication of being a social visionary or reformer. Most of Moczar's followers represent the younger generation of Party leaders, those who fought in the ranks during World War II, most of them as partisans in Poland.

Zbigniew Brzezinski wrote of them in 1965 that ". . . in a curious way [the] emerging new Polish communist elite resembles the pre-World War II extreme right-wing groups in Poland more than it resembles either its Comintern-reared Stalinist predecessors or the earlier, internationalist founders of the Polish Communist Party."[14]

However diverse in origin and persuasion, the Party's conservatives have coalesced sufficiently to spur increasingly repressive policies. Censorship has provided them with a common cause, and the purge of the Jews from public life with yet another.

In 1963 the Government suspended indefinitely the meetings of the famed discussion club, Krzywe Koło. This measure coincided with the replacement of the relatively liberal Edward Ochab by Ryszard Strzelecki as Head of the Party's Cultural Affairs section. The change was soon translated into other more stringent censorship measures. In March 1964 these brought forth a letter of protest addressed to Gomułka from thirty-four leading Polish writers and intellectuals. The Party's response was a series of reprisals against the signatories ranging from arrests to denial of passports for travel abroad. In April 1964 students at Warsaw University demonstrated against the regime; support and sympathy for the victims of the reprisals was also shown by the Polish Writers' Union. Considerable public resentment in Poland and even abroad became evident.

The Government relented to the extent of lifting restrictions on most of the thirty-four "offenders." But it imposed a ban on university-wide gatherings and its censorship practices continued to grow more harsh and stringent. In October 1964, Melchior Wańkowicz, a writer, was sentenced to three years imprisonment because of "offensive" remarks about the regime which he had made in a personal letter to his relatives in the United States. In March 1965 two teaching assistants at Warsaw University, Jacek Kuron and Karol Modzelewski, were expelled from the Party and given three-year jail terms for an open letter addressed to the PZPR, calling for a worker revolution to oust the current unresponsive, ruling Party bureaucracy. In September another writer, Jan Miller, drew an eighteen-month sentence for having published "false and damaging" statements about People's Poland in an émigré journal in London.

These actions led to renewed, and now obviously "illegal," demonstrations at Warsaw University and a cycle of regime reprisals against students in the latter part of 1965 and early 1966. In 1966 the Party expelled its own long time revisionist critic, Warsaw University philosophy professor Leszek Kolakowski. In 1967 still other writers and intellectuals were tried, expelled, and jailed.

In June 1967 reprisals connected with the issue of censorship merged with a major new campaign against "Zionism." Following the outbreak of Arab-Israeli conflict, Gomułka made a speech on June 19 in Warsaw in which he warned Polish Jews that the regime would not tolerate support for Israel among its citizens contrary to Poland's official pro-Soviet, pro-Arab policy. He told Jews that Poland would not permit a "fifth column in its midst."

The speech unloosened an avalanche which soon threatened Gomułka's own position in the Party. The Partisans and the Stalinists gleefully joined forces in behalf of a drastic purge of all Jews in sundry positions of responsibility and importance. Piasecki's *Słowo Powszechne* and organs favorable to Moczar such as *Żolnierz Wolności* (Soldier of Freedom) and *Prawo i Życie* (Law and Life) pictured a vast and dangerous Zionist conspiracy throughout the whole Polish body politic. The fact that the number of Jews in Poland had declined to some 20,000 persons out of a population of nearly 32 million, and that only one of fourteen members and deputy members of the Politburo (Eugeniusz Szyr) was Jewish did not deter them.

For the Stalinists this was an old technique. Their leaders, Nowak, Rokossovski, and Mijal, among others, took the same stance in October 1956. They presented the argument that the misfortunes and crimes of the 1945–1956 period were the result of the "misapplication of Communism" by Jews. Many Jews—Berman, Minc, Zambrowski, Różanski, and Fejgin—had occupied some of the highest positions in the Government and Party structures of Stalinist Poland; admittedly in mid-1956 most of the key Jewish figures were already gone. But the Stalinist panacea at the eleventh hour was simple and familiar enough: It is the Jews who are to blame.[15]

The slogan of removing Jews from important Party posts proved attractive to others as well. It was supported by Khrushchev himself in 1956. The Partisan group thus took over the Natolin program in this respect and has consistently sought to supplant persons of Jewish descent in the apparatus of power. The Arab-Israeli War provided it with an excellent opportunity to reap maximum advantage from this issue within the Party and, hopefully, throughout the country, too.

Notwithstanding the small number of Jews now remaining in Poland the racialist and anti-Semitic overtones of the Partisan outlook might well help their popularity. In the context of a highly influential half century of Dmowski's virulently anti-Semitic nationalism, the "Jewish issue" still possesses considerable residual appeal in Poland. Moczar and his allies called on Jews to publicly repudiate Zionism, demanded their ouster from the Party, and blamed them for a whole variety of misfortunes and alleged misfortunes of the past; they turned their attacks, however, also upon those who by their irresolution, hesitation or complicity had not acted against "Zionists." In March and April 1967, Gomułka and a few of his Party allies, notably Zenon Kliszko, attempted to slow down the anti-Semitic drive. But this proved quite ineffective. Party leaders long thought to be Gomułka's allies, particularly Gierek and Cyrankiewicz, seemed to ignore the First Secretary's admonitions that excesses must be avoided and that Zionism was not, after all, a major threat to the PZPR. On October 7, 1967 General Moczar made a television appearance in Warsaw in which he openly attacked Gomułka for his "half-measures" and inadequate handling of the "Zionist threat." By early 1968 several thousand Party and Government officials, university professors, scientists, newspaper editors, and military (among them at least three generals) had been ousted from their jobs with no indication that the purge would soon end. Not all of the victims were Jewish. Some Polish officials, lukewarm to the Arab cause or suspected of "liberal" leanings, appear to have been purged too.

The purge was given new impetus by student demonstrations in several Polish universities at the beginning of 1968. These had begun, traditionally enough, at Warsaw University in February in protest against a Government ban on a play by Mickiewicz (Dziady) critical of nineteenth-century Russian oppressors of Poland. In March, Moczar's militia arrested more than a thousand demonstrators in Warsaw, nearly 400 of them students. On March 10, ten students arrested earlier were given jail terms for "hooliganism and insulting the police."

On March 11, 1968 a crowd of workers and students sacked the Ministry of Culture Building in Warsaw, and serious rioting ensued with the police wielding clubs and tear gas against the surging crowds. Warsaw resounded to the shouts of "Long live Czechoslovakia!" and "Down with Censorship!"

Piasecki's *Słowo Powszechne* published the names of some of the Jewish student demonstrators as further evidence of Zionist activities against People's Poland and demanded that the youths' parents as well as the students themselves be punished.

The demands of a Warsaw University student organization, published in March 1968, reflected not only widespread popular aspirations, but also the poignant failure of Gomułka's regime to live up to the hopes of 1956.

The student declaration called on the regime to secure for the people the right of free association and discussion; allow full public disclosure of information about the economy and the functioning of the administration; enable public opinion to influence the determination of economic reforms; establish independent trade unions and workers' councils; abolish prior censorship; increase the role of the Sejm and give the public more information about pending legislation; respect the independence of the courts, and maintain civil rights, including the inviolability of persons, their homes and the mails; eliminate extra-legal punishments such as firing from jobs and denial of passports, and cease reprisals against courts and lawyers.[16]

On the eve of the Fifth National Congress of the PZPR, Gomułka appeared to be in the most serious straits since he took over the leadership in 1956. Having started the anti-Semitic campaign he seemed helpless to stop it. He and his followers were under constant attack from obviously powerful conservative forces within the Party. If there were any "liberals" or "revisionists" left in the Communist ranks in mid-1968 (and there obviously were) they seemed visible only in headlong retreat.

Gomułka's own pronouncements on the subject of anti-Semitism, his offer of exit visas to Jews, his hostile attitude to the Czech reformers, all seemed to indicate that if he did manage to contain the challenge to his leadership, it would be by embracing the outlook of his opponents.

Yet, the Party as a whole was profoundly estranged from the general opinion of the country. Economic difficulties had forced the regime to raise meat prices by 16.5 percent in November 1967, and consumer restrictions were once again compounding the political unrest. Even the usually persuasive appeal of anti-Semitism was muted and thwarted in 1967–68 by its unfortunate context, from the Party's point of view. The Soviet Union, after all, had backed the Arabs in the Mideast War with enormous material resources and all its diplomacy and propaganda. Israel's swift and decisive victory under these circumstances almost certainly delighted more Poles than it dismayed.

In August 1968, Gomułka virtually completed his transition from "rebellion" to "docility" toward Moscow, when he joined with the Russians, Hungarians, Bulgarians, and East Germans in the invasion of Czechoslovakia. Polish troops helped to destroy the liberal-reformist regime of their southern neighbor. For Gomułka and Poland, this was a great irony of history since, after all, in October 1956 it was Gomułka who had proclaimed and symbolized the right of the Polish people and implicitly of all peoples to determine their own fate. Apparently prepared to fight a Russian invasion of Poland in 1956, he assisted one against his Czechoslovak comrades some twelve years later. Gomułka's popularity at home clearly plummeted to a new low. Opposition, particularly from students and intellectuals, intensified. At the autumn Party Congress, the First Secretary's principal asset seemed to be Soviet backing. Appreciative of his loyalty to Moscow, Soviet officials, from Leonid Brezhnev down to the Soviet Ambassador in Warsaw, showered public praise on Gomułka. The challenge to his leadership from Moczar was temporarily thwarted, though clearly at the price of very repressive policies. In fact, for Moczar the Fifth Party Congress was not nearly a fiasco. The General advanced to membership in the sensitive Party Secretariat and also to candidate-membership in the Politburo. His rise to power seemed to have been slowed down rather than averted.

Gomułka's "anti-Zionist" campaign brought on an exodus of so many Polish Jews that in the words of Henryk Grynberg, "1968 was for Poland what 1492 was for Spain—the year of expulsion". [17] Thousands of Jews, most of the remaining 20,000, many of them barely identified with Judaism except through birth, were forced into exile in

1968–1970: accused of disloyalty, fired from their jobs, forced into humiliating public denunciations of Zionism and the state of Israel, and stripped of their possessions on departure.

Among Polish Jews finding refuge in Denmark was Dr. Juliusz Katz-Suchy, erstwhile ambassador of People's Poland to the United Nations, and more recently professor of international law at Warsaw University. More than ten thousand party members were expelled for a variety of "sins" including wrong lineage.

In another demonstration of toughness, the regime ousted in 1968 the only member of the Roman Catholic "opposition" in the Council of State—Jerzy Zawieyski of *Znak*. General Wojciech Jaruzelski, a Moczar sympathizer, replaced Gomulka's personal confidante, Marshal Marian Spychalski, as Minister of Defense. Early in 1969 two leaders of the student protest movement, Jacek Kuron and Karol Modzelewski, received new three-and-a-half -year jail sentences for allegedly instigating the 1968 student uprising.

In 1970 the legacy of repression was compounded by striking economic failure. Even before the regime had issued its catastrophic December 13 price-increase decree, Poland was simultaneously beset by inflation and unemployment much worse than those of her communist neighbors. The pent-up frustrations of the Polish people, particularly the workers, found expression in the wave of strikes and riots that began in the Baltic coast ports of Gdynia, Szczecin, and Gdansk. The riots are variously estimated to have caused between forty and eighty deaths and several hundred lesser casualties, as thousands of people clashed with the police and the military.* In several towns and cities Party headquarters and State buildings were attacked and set on fire by surging crowds of demonstrators. Large segments of the Polish industrial economy were brought to a standstill. In some locations, workers threatened to destroy plants and machinery. The disturbances spread to other parts of Poland, including Warsaw, Łódź, and Poznań, where they vividly recalled the bloody events of 1956. Polish police and troops, backed by tanks, repeatedly fired on strikers and demonstrators.

Although the regime's intitial response to the strikes and riots of 1970 was unyielding in the best traditions of pre-1956 Stalinism, Gomułka resigned from his post within seven days at the December 20th meeting of the PZPR Central Committee. Unlike the events of 1956, no massive disclosures of party infighting that must have led to

---

*According to an official Party report of June 1971, 45 persons died and 1,165 were injured, 19 "public buildings" were destroyed, and 220 stores looted.

Gomułka's departure have yet been made. Soviet armored units in East Germany and the USSR were widely reported deploying for occupation of the country during the chaotic week of December 13–20. Clearly, unless the Polish Communists could hold on to power under *some* acceptably orthodox form of leadership, the Soviet Union was prepared to invoke the Brezhnev Doctrine. "Socialism" in Poland would be "rescued" by Soviet forces just as it had been, with Poland's help, in August 1968 in Czechoslovakia and by Russians alone in November 1956 in Hungary.

Sacrificing Gomułka to mass discontent, the Party turned to Edward Gierek, a man with a reputation as a successful, pragmatic manager. The liberator of 1956 had become the oppressor of 1970. Many of the charges leveled at Gomułka by his successors ironically echoed the accusations against the Stalinists of the 1950s: authoritarianism, aloofness, disregard of popular needs and wishes, lack of dialogue, bureaucratization, arbitrariness, and the like.

If the Polish people may be said to have cried out for bread and freedom in December 1970, this was not a propitious moment to install General Moczar in power. In fact, the police repression with which Moczar was identified and which he was applying failed to produce a solution. Violence and disorder were growing not declining. But even though Moczar did not succeed Gomułka in the December Revolution, Moczar's presence heavily tinged any promise of liberalization that Gierek held out.

The pattern of personnel changes under the Gierek regime was by no means clear. In the wake of Gomulka's departure, Moczar advanced to full membership in the Politburo and was given Cabinet rank in the government of Piotr Jaroszewicz. His close ally, Franciszek Świtała, was named Minister of the Interior in January 1971. No less ominously, an old hard-line, Władyslaw Kruczek, was named by Gierek to succeed Loga-Sowiński as head of the Trade Unions. But, within six months, Świtała was fired along with several less officials of the Ministry of Interior. Moczar himself remained mysteriously out of public view in April and May of 1971, with conflicting rumors circulating in Warsaw that he was "merely" suffering from a heart ailment and that he had been purged. In June he was named Chairman of the Supreme Chamber of Control—an agency charged with auditing the work of all government organs. Simultaneously, however, Moczar was relieved of his post in the politically sensitive Secretariat of the Party's Central Committee. Party leaders in areas hardest hit by the December 1970 violence, including Gdansk, Sczczecin, Łódź, Warsaw and Lublin were fired. But the unsavory hard-liner and Moczar ally, Bolesław Piasecki, was elevated to Cabinet rank. The appointment of Vice Premier Krasko to supervise cultural policies on the government side seemed a "liberal" move but was apparently offset by the assignment of "conservative" Stefan Olszowski to the management of cultural policy within the Politburo. A general purge of rank-and-file "opportunists" in the Party was announced and begun in 1971.

On the other hand, Gierek's policy initiatives in the fields of economics, censorship, Church-State relations, and procedures adopted for the Party's Sixth National Congress in December 1971, all involved liberalization. The regime publicized a so-called Consumer's Charter, pledging to link output increases in industrial goods with price cuts; devote more effort to consumer research; increase the availability of cheaper products; and, in particular, to maintain a two-year freeze on the prices of non-seasonal goods, especially foodstuffs. Gierek placated Polish workers by abandoning his predecessor's incentive plan. The aborted plan geared workers' incomes to productivity increases and caused widespread fears of wage cuts and unemployment. The regime promised to improve health care and other social services for the general population, through increased taxation of Poland's relatively modest private economic sector. The new Five-Year Plan submitted for approval of the Sixth Congress emphasized consumer priorities, housing, and the development of light industry. Investment and credit policies toward private farming were eased, too.

Cultural policies pursued at the height of the anti-Zionist campaign were relaxed. The regime permitted the publication of works by authors such as Stefan Kisielewski and Ryszard Gontarz, banned since 1968. It also allowed the publication of works by persons of Jewish descent, such as the late Antoni Słonimski. Church- State contacts were dramatized by "a summit conference" between Cardinal Wyszyński and Premier Jaroszewicz in March and the subsequent transfer of ownership of some 7000 church buildings in the Oder-Neisse territories by the government to the Polish Church. Talk of a papal visit to Poland was revived in 1971. And Gierek promised to make the Party Congress more responsive to non-party "expert" opinion than ever before.

The new officialdom of Gierek's regime reflected greater emphasis upon technocrats and managers rather than ideologues, revolutionists, and the military. In this respect, the Polish Revolution of 1970 produced results already observed elsewhere in Eastern Europe.[18] General Moczar and his allies, as manipulators of violence, could be regarded as anachronisms. At the December Party Congress, Moczar was, in fact, removed from the Politburo, but the conservative wing of the PZPR as a whole remained strong. An old Stalinist, Stefan Misia-szek, became chief of the Party's Central Control Commission. Jaruzel-ski, Kruczek, Olszowski, and Szlachcic were elected to Gierek's eleven-man Politburo with Józef Kępa one of four candidate members. Bolesław Rumiński became a member of the Council of State; he joined two other "hard liners," Wiktor Kłosiewicz and Władysław Kruczek in the leadership of the Trade Unions. Stalinist Zenon Nowak became Gierek's new ambassador to Moscow. The Party's course was thus far from settled in 1972.

NOTES

1. The first part of this chapter is based largely on the data of Richard F. Staar, *Poland 1944–1962: The Sovietization of a Captive People* (Baton Rouge, La., 1962), and M. K. Dziewanowski, *The Communist Party of Poland: An Outline of History* (Cambridge, Mass., 1959). See also Stehle, *op. cit.*, and *Rocznik Statystyczny*, Głowny Urząd Statystyczny, Warsaw, 1962–1967 volumes; Hiscocks, *op. cit.*

2. See Andrzej Korboński, "The Polish Communist Party 1938–1942," *Slavic Review*, vol. XXVI, no. 3, September 1967, pp. 430–444.

3. See Staar, *op. cit.*, p. 180; cf. Stehle, *op. cit.*, pp. 24–25.

4. For Bierut's version of communism–and quarrel with Gomułka's revisionism–see his *O. Partii* (Warsaw, 1952). See also Adam Ulam, *Titoism and the Cominform* (Cambridge, Mass. 1952).

5. Dziewanowski, *op. cit.*, p. 255; D. Healey (ed.), *The Story of the Socialists in Eastern Europe* (London, 1951); "R," "The Fate of Polish Socialism," *Foreign Affairs*, XXVIII, October 1949, pp. 125–142.

6. See S. L. Sharp, *New Constitutions in the Soviet Sphere*, (Washington D.C., 1950). Cf. Stanisław Stroński, *Spór o dwie Konstytucje* (A Quarrel About Two Constitutions) (London, 1941).

7. See W. Gomułka, *Przemówienia* (Speeches) Ksiazka i Wiedza: Warsaw, 1963. Interesting Gomułka recollections of war time Polish Communism appeared in his speech commemorating the twentieth anniversary of the original PPR on January 20, 1962 in Warsaw, pp. 7–41.

8. S. Rosada and J. Gwóźdź, *Forced Labor and Confinement Without Trial in Poland*, Washington D.C., National Committee for a Free Europe, 1952; Leland Stowe, *Conquest by Terror: The Story of Satellite Europe*, New York, 1952.

9. On this see especially Konrad Syrop, *Spring in October* (New York, 1957), p. 52.

10. Paul E. Zinner (ed.), *National Communism and Popular Revolt in Eastern Europe: A Selection of Documents On Events in Poland and Hungary, February-November 1956* (New York, 1956), pp. 67–84; 197–239.

11. Leopold Labedz, "Leszek Kolakowski, or Ethics and Communism," *Survey*, No. 23, January-March 1958, pp. 71–79; L. Labedz (ed.), *Revisionism* (New York, 1962). Cf. Michael Gamarnikov, "Poland: Political Pluralism in a One-Party State," *Problems of Communism*, vol. XVI, no. 4, July-August 1967, pp. 1–14; H. Gordon Skilling, "The Party, Opposition and Interest Groups: Fifty Years of Continuity and Change," *International Journal*, vol. XXII, no. 4, Autumn 1967, pp. 618–31.

12. Adam Ciołkosz, "Marxism and the Individual," *East Europe*, vol. 15, no. 5, May 1966, pp. 16–22.

13. The record of the Central Committee's extensive debate on the book is contained in *Nowe Drogi*, vol. 12, no. 199, December 1965, pp. 57–186.

14. *Alternative to Partition* (New York, 1965), p. 32. See also Romuald Barwicz, "UB a sowiecka służba bezpieczeństwa" *Kultura* (Paris) no. 6/273, June 1970, pp. 70–100. Barwicz believes that Moczar is really a crucial Soviet agent-confidante in Poland ("wtyczka") who personally controls the Security Police organization on behalf of the Russians. Barwicz points out that the UB has been greatly strengthened and revived since 1956, particularly in the 1965–70 period.

15. On this theme see S. L. Schneiderman, *Warsaw Heresy* (New York, 1959).

16. See "Deklaracja Ruchu Studenckiego w Polsce" *Kultura* (Paris) no. 10/252, October 1968, pp. 87–91.

17. See his "Wygnanie z Polski" *Kultura* (Paris) No. 11/254, November 1968, p.49 and pp.49–54.

18. See Carl Beck, "Career Characteristics of East European Leadership", pp.157–194 in R. Barry Farrell, (ed.) *Political Leadership in Eastern Europe and the Soviet Union* (Chicago, 1970).

4

The Red and the
Black: Communism
and Catholicism

THE CAPABILITIES OF the Communist regime and the policy and administrative "outputs" which are produced by the system are affected in various ways by the activities of the Church. The regime's capacity for regulating the behavior or the political-ideological disposition of the citizens; the capacity for the allocation and distribution of resources; the capacity for evoking symbolic manifestations; the capacity to recruit and socialize individuals into the political system: in all these, secular and religious activities intertwine.[1] As indicated earlier, Catholicism has been significantly identified with Polish politics and Polish nationalism for centuries.

The Church was, on the whole, closely identified with the pre-war authoritarian and right-wing Polish regime, but, in keeping with traditions, it also established an excellent record of resistance to Nazism during the Second World War. Almost a fifth of the Polish clergy perished in Nazi concentration camps and before firing squads. As so often before, the Church shared in the martyrdom of the whole nation. After the war the position of the Church, however threatened by Communist atheism or Communist measures, became actually even stronger in certain respects than it was before 1939.

Partly, this was a result of the now almost wholly Catholic make-up of the population. More than a matter of numbers, however, the power of the Church has been buttressed by the piety and the religious commitment of a very substantial portion of the people, a great majority of whom are regular church-goers and practicing Catholics.

Before the war—under the Concordat of 1925—the Church was largely maintained by state salaries and possessed extensive landholdings. Since the war it has continued to retain some of its income from the state in the form of salaries for religious instruction to children and

80

for other priestly services rendered in public institutions of People's Poland. What the Church has lost in landholdings—through Communist land reforms—has been more than made up by the volunatry contributions of the Polish people. Thus, in 1968 the Church had some sixty-nine bishops where there were only forty-five before 1939. There were about 18,000 parish priests where there were only about 10,000 in 1939. There have been more monks and students of theology than in the prewar period. The number of nuns has risen from 12,000 to nearly 30,000. There are at least three churches in operation in Poland today for every two in 1939.* Even in publishing, where Church press organs have suffered some diminution, a formidable influence remains. There are today some fifty Catholic publications in existence with a total weekly and monthly circulation of about 600,000 copies. The Church maintains its own University at Lublin and 48 Theological Seminaries throughout the country. As of 1968, the Church dispensed Catholic instruction to school-age children at some 16,000 so-called "catechism-posts."

The Church episcopate has been led by a formidable figure—Stefan Cardinal Wyszyński. The Cardinal, born in 1901 of peasant ancestry, succeeded to his present post in the Polish episcopate in 1948. Before the war, Wyszyński was a canon law scholar and also something of a social reformer, interested in trade unionism and the improvement of the material welfare of the workers and the poor. He was active in the resistance movement against the Nazis. After the war the Cardinal attempted to achieve a practical *modus vivendi* with the new Communist regime.

This led to the agreement of April 14, 1950 between the Government and the episcopate. The key provisions guaranteed the Church freedom of religous teaching, in and out of the public school system, and protection for religious observances and Church publications. It also gave pledges of financial support to the Church in payment for a variety of religious services in institutions like hospitals, schools, prisons, and in the armed forces. In return, the Church leadership undertook to "oppose the abuse of religious sentiments for anti-state purposes"; submit to the legal constitutional order of People's Poland, and loyally support the reconstruction of the country. Moreover, the Church promised to work actively for the permanent incorporation of the lands east of the Oder-Neisse line into Poland, and against all "revisionist" (presumably West-German) attempts to prevent this. It

---

*Church spokesmen discount at least some of these gains on the ground that the increases do not match the growth of Poland's Catholic population since 1939.

also went on record in support of the principle "that the Pope is the
. . . supreme authority [in] matters of religion, morality and church
jurisdiction, but in other matters the episcopate will be guided by
Polish *raison d'état.*"

The 1950 pact outwardly appeared advantageous to both sides but
the maintenance of widespread cultural and educational influence by
the Church, even in return for its diplomatic and political support, was
untenable for Poland's Communist regime at the height of the Stalinist
sovietization of Europe. What the regime granted on paper it attempted to deny in practice. An ideological coexistence with Catholicism was, in fact, unacceptable to it in the long run. Even then,
however, the attack on religion in Poland was not openly and directly
turned upon the institution of the Church or upon any of its spiritual
tenets and teachings. A frontal assault of this sort would have been far
too dangerous for the regime to attempt, probably no less serious than
forced collectivization. The Communists resorted, instead, to selective
harassments of the Church on a large scale, and even to its subversion
through officially inspired "progressive catholicism."

Like other Communist regimes, the Polish one chose the charges of
espionage, treason, and corruption as its public indictments of individual Church leaders. In the 1950s hundreds of priests were jailed by the
security police. In 1951 the bishop of Kielce, Kaczmarek, was put in
jail and kept there for two years before being brought to trial on
trumped up espionage charges. He was alleged to have been in the
service of the United States. In September 1953 Cardinal Wyszyński
was arrested—without charges—and kept in secret confinement until
the October 1956 revolution when, with equal blandness, he was
released.

When at last the "thaw" began in earnest, a new Church-State
agreement was drafted in December 1956. It was a substantial renewal
of the mutual cooperation pledges of 1950. In the years which have
elapsed since then, however, the Church-Party conflict has gone on in
various forms from one crisis to another.

Gomułka's relations with the Church were punctuated by recurrent
clashes and mutual accusations. The Church periodically renewed its
charges against the Party for seeking to limit, deny, and destroy the
Church's right to teach, to operate its institutions, and to hold public
religious observances. The Party accused the Church of exploiting
religion for political purposes and of disloyalty to the state.

Thus there has been continued Church-Party conflict in Poland over
education. Until 1955 religious instruction was supplied by Church
designated instructors, at government expense, in all public and sec-

ondary schools. It even enjoyed the status of required course work. In 1955 it was barred altogether and then restored on an optional basis by Gomułka in 1957 only for those children whose parents addressed a written request for it. About 95 percent of the parents apparently opted for religious instruction for their children. As a result, there turned out to be only 120 out of some seventeen thousand schools in People's Poland without a program of religious teaching!

Alarmed by the strength of the Church in the schools, the Party banned all religious instruction *within* school premises but allowed it outside in 1960. It also attempted to subject to its control and to restrain such extra-mural religious teaching by the controversial Education Act of 1961. This law provided for Ministry of Education scrutiny of all the extra-mural instructional facilities. It set up a demanding and rigid building code for Church schools and required priests who gave instruction to register with the Government. Cardinal Wyszyński openly pronounced the law unacceptable and implicitly exterminatory. Most priests defied Government regulations, and the Party temporarily gave up on its attempt to undermine the Church's role in education.

The overtly political significance of the Church was illustrated in 1956–57 when Gomułka asked its help in assuring popular support for his new regime. In 1957 the Church responded to the Government's call for a massive turn-out at the polls. Led by Cardinal Wyszyński, it gave its tacit support to the candidates of the Front of National Unity. In all subsequent local and national elections in 1958, 1961, 1965, and 1969, the regime has made special appeals to Catholics for their votes; in doing so it has attempted to define the obligations of citizenship in People's Poland in such a way as to make religion and politics separate and reconcilable realms. The Party professed to distinguish between "good" Catholics who were also law-abiding citizens for whom it professed sympathetic understanding, and the "bad" Catholics who were using religion for political purposes as tools of treason and reaction.

The basic unwillingness of the Party to acquiesce in the maintenance, let alone expansion, of the Church's influence led to generally worsening political relations in the past decade. The brief thaw of 1956–57 ended when it became apparent that Gomułka was not really prepared to reverse the religious policies of his predecessors. These policies have included closing down church schools and institutions; assorted obstruction of religious education generally; interference with church processions and public observances; disruptive drafting of theological students into the armed forces; refusal to issue building permits for the construction of churches, church schools, and institutions. Moreover, the government was unwilling to liquidate its Catholic "front organization," *Pax*, which the Cardinal had denounced in July 1957. Early in 1958 the government press was charging that village priests, *en masse*, were stirring up "intolerance of non-believers" among the peasants and attempting the "moral isolation" of the Communist Party in the countryside. Priests were being accused of encouraging the faithful to break the laws. In May, a suspended jail sentence was meted out to a priest who, in a widely publicized altercation, refused to bury the body of a local Communist official in the consecrated grounds of the cemetery in the town of Zuronin. The priest was found guilty of inciting the population to riot. In an unprecedented act of sacrilege and political reprisal, Polish security police carried out a "search and seizure" operation at the monastery of Poland's holiest Catholic shrine of Jasna Góra in July. Today Poland's principal religous shrine, Jasna Góra at Częstochowa derives its fame from the resistance offered there to a Swedish invasion in 1655. The brutality of the incursion provoked widespread resentment among Polish Catholics and brought protests from Cardinal Wyszyński and the whole Polish episcopate. In September 1958 the Government's attempt to remove crosses from school classrooms led to mass protests by parents and gave the Communists a convincing demonstration of the strength of popular sentiment behind religion and the Church in Poland.

In 1959 and 1960 the Government continued to follow a policy of selective crackdowns against priests, occassionally bringing them to trial on a variety of compromising charges and generally meting out short prison terms and suspended sentences. Thus, in January 1959 one priest was tried for involvement in black market activities and in early 1960 another one was tried for "intimidating" teachers who propagated atheism. In November 1959 the Government waged an unsuccessful campaign for the removal of the bishop of Kielce, Kaczmarek, whom it had jailed in 1951. He was now accused of "anti-state activity" and wartime collaboration with the Nazis. The Church publicly denied the regime's right to remove a bishop from office and despite the regime's refusal to recognize the very existence of a bishop of Kielce, the Church steadfastly supported him.

In 1962 the episcopate asked for a Sejm inquiry into the persecution of the Church by the regime but the request was promptly, and predictably, refused. The Government press accused Cardinal Wyszyński of seeking to create an "aura of persecution and martyrdom" in order to bolster the public position of the Church. This seemed hardly necessary in view of the repeated evidences of massive popular support for it in all parts of Poland.

Beyond an outspoken self-defense, the Church has also taken the initiative in condemning those actions of the regime which offend its conception of a religious-moral stewardship of the nation. Cardinal Wyszyński has repeatedly condemned atheism and has prayed for the return to the fold of the "fallen," i.e., of Communist non-believers. He has vigorously condemned the use of tax funds for the purpose of spreading atheism. He has condemned Government experiments with birth control. In defending the freedom of Polish Catholics, the Cardinal and the Polish episcopate have clearly and repeatedly identified their own particular claims with those of the whole Polish nation.

The regime's charge that the Church has injected itself into politics is not without foundation, if for no other reason than that the Polish people, deprived of most secular channels for voicing grievances and opposition, have done so through the Church. In the absence of genuinely competing political parties, the Church has taken on additional "interest articulation" or "representational" functions within the political system. Thus virtually every act and pronouncement of the priesthood have had their political dimensions. Religious hymns sung in churches, the processions and enthusiastic shouts of "Niech żyje," (Long Live) greeting Cardinal Wyszyński on his travels through Poland have been in large measure political as well as religious phenomena: they have been manifestations of a national resolve to hold out against Communism. Rarely was this evidenced more clearly and directly than during Poland's millennium celebrations of 1966.

These began with a series of accusations and administrative restrictions levelled against the Church by the regime, ostensibly in reprisal for its interference in Poland's foreign affairs. In November 1965 a pastoral letter directed by the Polish to the West German episcopate was seized upon by the government as proof of the Church's allegedly treasonable willingness to "give away" Poland's western frontiers.

Reprisals ensued. Cardinal Wyszyński was denied a visa to travel to Rome and the United States as he had planned. Government organs renewed earlier charges that he had in the past consorted with anti-regime London exiles. He was descirbed as a hardened enemy of communism, of People's Poland, and even as an erstwhile fascist. A projected visit by Pope Paul VI was quashed by the Government and led the Pontif to a public statement of regret and reproach directed clearly at Poland's rulers. Visas were denied to scores of western churchmen whom the Cardinal had invited to help celebrate Poland's millennium. A variety of restrictions on pilgrimages and tourist travel were imposed within Poland to discourage Church-sponsored observances. Processions (including the Cardinal's own car on some occasions) were sporadically detained by the police. The regime attempted to counter the millennium's religious significance and activities with political rallies of its own and diversionary entertainment such as football games and motorcycle and bicycle racing meets.

These measures proved almost wholly unavailing. In the confrontation between Polish Communism and Polish Catholicism the latter was an overwhelming winner. The most dramatic confrontations took place in Kraków, in May, when Premier Cyrankiewicz held an outdoor rally to commemorate the traditional workers' holiday on May 1st. With all the urging of police and administrative agencies for maximum participation, some 150,000 persons from the city and its environs rather quietly and reservedly took part. But on May 3, the anniversary of the Polish reform Constitution of 1791, Cardinal Wyszyński, celebrating mass in Kraków, was greeted by over half a million cheering, enthusiastic Poles lining the streets, a number actually in excess of the city's total population! The government suffered a similar setback when in June a confrontation between the Cardinal and Gomułka occurred in Poznań. The Cardinal's sermon drew an overflow, voluntary audience which clung to rooftops and treetops in the vicinity of the church. Gomułka spoke to groups of workers marched and driven from nearby plants, and disconcertedly observed his captive audience melt as it wandered off to hear more stimulating fare in another part of town.

In celebrating the millennium, Cardinal Wyszyński boldly emphasized themes which were bound to distress the regime. He publicly asserted that after one thousand years Poland was and had a right to be a Catholic nation, that this was the significance of her millennium. He asserted that the freedom of the Church was also the freedom of the whole nation. The Party was bound to react sharply to such an overt challenge to its authority, but its evident failure to arouse public enthusiasm and support simply served to expose its weakness.

The struggle for men's loyalties between Church and Party in Poland has see-sawed in almost every field of public concern. The Party has had the advantage of wielding the governmental machine. The Church has dominated the loyalties of public opinion. In the 1960s, after more than twenty years of Communist rule, there appeared to be many more believers and practicing Catholics among Party members than out-and-out atheists. In the population at large the balance was even more grotesquely one-sided. Where Communist meetings, with all the advantages of bureaucratic manipulation, draw meager crowds, religious pilgrimages draw hundreds of thousands of people in all parts of Poland.

More than likely, the religiosity of the Polish people has been significantly augmented by secular-political factors. Attendance at church and religious festivals has become a manifestation of opposition to Communism, a rallying round the one, large, public, visible and irreconcilable symbol of resistance to Communist control. This national-political aspect of Polish Catholicism lends substance to the fears of Church leaders that religious life in Poland, as elsewhere, is not immune to trends of increasing materialism and this-worldliness, particularly among the younger generation. Would the church's power actually decline if Communist rule crumbled? This may be a moot question. The sober fact remains that all accommodations between Church and Party in Poland have been clearly limited by a doctrinal chasm which neither side is willing to bridge or repudiate.

Time and again the two sides have publicly agreed to coexist; each in its proper sphere, and each with a view to obvious practical advantages. The Communists could not disregard the power of public opinion and the Church appreciated the significance of financial, administrative, and police controls exercised by the state. Each side could gain something by the benevolence of the other. Ultimately, however, the Communists could not permanently "coexist with God" and the Church would hardly acquiesce in the conversion of its believers to the tenets of Marxism-Leninism. An ideological victory for the latter would be tantamount to the Church's own extinction. Repeated declarations and pledges of loyalty and cooperation have been treated with mistrust by both sides.

An important factor in the behavior of the Party and of the Church, as indeed of almost everyone in Poland, has been the anticipation of Soviet attitudes. Under the leadership of Cardinal Wyszyński, the Church's position in Poland has always been one of outward submission to the regime. In fact, the Cardinal had pioneered a policy which recognized that the power and the proximity of the USSR made some form of "Communism" a permanent feature on the Polish scene, that the Soviet Union was not likely to tolerate the overthrow of Communist rule on its doorstep, and that a struggle against it might well bring about far worse evils than some form of accommodation. When Gomułka told Polish voters in 1957 that to cross out Communist candidates from the ballots was to cross out Poland's name from the map of Europe, he was stating a view which had been implicitly accepted by the Cardinal as well. [2]

Cardinal Wyszyński's policy sought to insure the survival of the

Church and of its influence without posing open challenges to the Party's rule. It has also backed the Party in behalf of the permanent incorporation of the western lands into Poland. In both respects—the policy of accommodation and the Oder-Neisse frontier—Cardinal Wyszyński followed a particularly difficult course during the papacy of Pius XII. The Vatican did not, in fact, agree to the Cardinal's recommendation for the establishment of five permanent Polish bishoprics in the former German areas. When Wyszynski visited Rome in 1957 to receive his Cardinal's hat he was apparently treated with marked coolness by Pius XII, to whom any kind of *modus vivendi* with communism was profoundly unpalatable.

On the other hand, the regime has bitterly resented the Vatican's failure to recognize the permanence of the new Polish-German frontiers. Its hopes for such recognition did not materialize during the papacy of John XXIII (1958–1963) and appear to have been dashed by his death. Communist propaganda has assiduously cultivated an image of John XXIII as a model "coexistence" pope, in contrast with his allegedly reactionary, rabidly anti-communist, and pro-Western predecessor, Pius XII, and his current successor, Paul VI.

But Cardinal Wyszyński's role has also changed in consequence of the events since 1956. His hopes that Gomułka would somehow inaugurate a "hands-off-religion" policy after the October Revolution had been profoundly disappointed. The Cardinal's defense of the Church and his criticisms of the regime had earned him its bitter enmity. Particularly since the Church-State confrontations of the 1966 millennium the Cardinal has been the target of vicious attacks by the Communist communications media and had become a virtual *persona non grata* to the regime.

When Pope Paul appointed archbishop Karol Wojtyla of Kraków Cardinal in 1967 this gave rise to wide-ranging speculation that the Papacy was thereby preparing another, more acceptable channel of communication with the regime. The Party press encouraged this speculation by picturing the new Cardinal as a "progressive" and a "patriot," unlike his reactionary senior colleague, the Primate of Poland, Cardinal Wyszyński.

When General de Gaulle visited Poland in 1967 he carefully avoided meeting Cardinal Wyszyński. This gesture was widely interpreted as part of his effort not to offend Gomułka and woo Poland towards France and away from the Soviet Union. But when subsequently, in the course of his tour of Poland, the General visited the historic Cathedral at Wawel in Kraków, it turned out that Cardinal Wojtyla was much too busy to greet the President of France in the seat of his ecclesiastical jurisdiction.

In addition to the Catholic Church there are several important groups which claim to represent Catholic opinion and have varying degrees of affiliation with Church hierarchy. The group closest to the Church is *Znak* (Sign), an association of Catholic intelligentsia with six representatives in the 1969 Sejm, led for the past several years by Jerzy Zawieyski.

The *Znak* group is undoubtedly the closest approximation to a legal opposition party under Communist rule anywhere, with the possible exception of Czechoslovakia in 1968. To be sure, this opposition, like that of the Church, confines itself to fairly narrow ground. *Znak* is a preeminently "loyal opposition." It is not only committed to open, legal, and peaceful action, but also accepts the inevitability, if not the desirability, of a Communist regime in Poland and dedicates itself to a pragmatic amelioration of conditions under red rule. It works for the extension of religious and individual freedom, the upholding of the rule of law, and it hopes to maintain a cultural and ideological pluralism within a Communist ruled-state. It is neither anti-regime nor anti-Soviet. It does not advocate the rooting out of Marxism in Poland. But it defends the Church and Catholicism. It strives for a more liberal society under the shield of a People's Democracy which Soviet-domination and international circumstances make unavoidable. Above all, it has done so publicly in the Sejm, in its press and public meetings. *Znak* is numerically very small—by no means a mass organization. Its Catholic Intelligentsia Clubs are confined to just five major cities in Poland, with about a thousand members in all. Its financial support comes from its publications and a private cosmetics and haberdashery business which the Government allows it to operate. Its significance stems partly from its elite character, partly from its ties to the top Church hierarchy and also its access to various institutions and personalities of the regime and significantly also from its role of "virtual representation." As a *de facto* legal opposition *Znak* is widely perceived to be representative of far wider circles of Polish opinion than its modest membership would indicate. Its protests and admonitions are not taken lightly by the regime.

Another interesting and important group with Catholic affiliations is *Caritas*, a mixed body of priests and laymen which is heavily subsidized by Government funds and which runs a variety of welfare institutions throughout Poland. These include hospitals, old people's homes, and clinics. They employ several thousand persons including about 600 priests and more than 2000 nuns. Until 1956 *Caritas* was under the direction of the *Pax* group discussed below. Today, *Caritas* finds a political expression in a small Christian-Social Association led by Jan Frankowski with three seats in the 1969 Sejm. This group is far more subservient to the regime than *Znak*. Dr. Frankowski has actually devoted some of his time to denouncing *Znak* and other Catholic organizations for lack of zeal in their support of the regime. On the other hand, even this more overtly "collaborationist" Catholic group has been a mixed blessing to the Party. For despite its elaborate avowals of "civic responsibility" and "support for the social system of People's Poland," *Caritas* has helped to maintain a significant cultural and ideological Catholic influence in a broad spectrum of public institutions. It has been an *ipso facto* counterweight to the eroding Marxist-Leninist influences.

Finally, there has also been a group of Catholic collaborators which in its devious attempt to become a pillar of Poland's Communist regime has earned the open disapprobation of the Church. The latter is the *Pax* society organized in 1945 by Bolesław Piasecki for the express purpose of winning over Catholics to the support of the regime. The *Pax* society is in many ways a strange paradox.[3]

Its founder and current leader was a prominent fascist chieftain in pre-war Poland, the leader of the so-called Falanga, a close imitation of the German Nazi party. Systematic violence against Jews, physical and verbal, and the aspiration to an iron-clad nationalist dictatorship for Poland were its most distinctive features. The group had a highly vocal, though relatively small, following among the Polish middle class and university youths. In the 1930s Piasecki appeared to be an aspiring Polish Fuehrer. During the Second World War his hopes for collaboration with the Nazis, and the role of a Polish Quisling, were dashed by Hitler's determination to make Poland a wholly German possession. There was no "deal" that Piasecki could make for himself and his group under Hitler's rule. Piasecki reluctantly turned to resistance— against both Germans and Russians. In 1944 and 1945 Piasecki's guerrillas dispatched many a Red Army man to his death. In 1945 Piasecki was arrested by Soviet security police but somehow suffered neither death nor even prolonged imprisonment. He appears to have persuaded the Russians that he could be more useful to them alive than dead. According to some accounts he became a direct Soviet agent. In any event, Piasecki became a significant political influence on behalf of Communist rule in a nation singularly lacking in Communists.

Piasecki was not only "allowed" to organize his pro-Communist Catholic society, *Pax,* but also given ample funds and provided with a daily newspaper, *Słowo Powszechne.* Over the years, he has built a multimillion commercial empire for himself connected with his own publishing firm, also under the name *Pax*. This firm has become Poland's second largest publishing house. Piasecki's publishing and other commercial enterprises provide jobs for his supporters and serve as outlets for his propaganda. *Pax* exists as a strange monument to private enterprise—economic and political—in a Communist land. One of *Pax*'s more legitimate contributions has been the publication of translated works of western literature, including the works of some non-Communists and anti-Communists. One *Pax* subsidiary, *Veritas*, produces some 40 percent of all religious articles sold in Poland.

In 1955 Piasecki managed to bring upon himself the open condemnation of the Vatican. Some of his publications were placed on the papal index of prohibited works, and Piasecki retreated before this pressure. He withdrew from circulation publications condemned by the Vatican including his controversial book, *Essential Problems*. While Piasecki has been for years a *persona non grata* to Cardinal Wyszyński, he has continued to play the role of a spokesman for Catholic *lay* opinion and seek political converts among priests.

In doing this, Piasecki has made it difficult for the Polish Church to officially counteract his activities. To do so, the Church would have to become more publicly anti-Communist, anti-Soviet, and overtly "political" than it might wish or could be. With some adroitness, Piasecki has managed to establish an ideological and political identity which distinguishes him and his group from the Communists, and yet does not prevent him from becoming the most pro-Soviet figure in Polish public life since 1945. Piasecki's redefinition of Catholicism has included the secular duty to advance the victory of Soviet Communism and "socialist construction" not only in Poland but throughout the World.

In practice, *Pax* has supported virtually all Communist policies at home and abroad, including attacks on the Vatican ("agency of American Imperialism") and the imprisonment of Polish bishops ("spies and agents"). Piasecki's rationale in the latter case was that the bishops had departed from the true faith in behaving as the regime alleged that they had. Even in the period of his avid subservience to Stalinism, Piasecki was operating on a platform of national-patriotic interest which identified communism as the "wave of the future," and insurance against revival of Pan-Germanism in the West. It was desirable for Poles to join in this enterprise which was destined to sweep the world. Piasecki has affected to believe that Communist institutions and ideals are not only compatible with Catholicism but desirable secular vehicles for a Catholic spirituality. Somewhat like the great erstwhile leader of

Polish nationalism, Roman Dmowski, Piasecki was advocating collaboration with Russia—on a much grander scale—from the otherwise appealing premises of national self-interest, patriotism, and even religion.

Piasecki has succeeded in developing his own brand of "black bolshevism" in Poland. He has gained some former nationalists, reactionaries and fascists to the "patriotic cause of Communism." He has been an ideological ally and supporter of General Moczar and a leading proponent of the so-called anti-Zionist campaign since 1967. What renders his *Pax* movement of special interest is that Piasecki has exacted a relatively high price for his collaborationism, ideologically, organizationally, and financially within the framework of a Communist regime. Thus, his numerically small group (probably under 3000 members) along with *Znak* and the Christian Social Association, is a participant in the Front of National Unity through which the regime presents candidates and programs to the voters. It has been a force of influence in Polish politics, particularly in the behind-the-scenes politics of State administration. Even in the heyday of Stalinism, the security police and the judiciary have been known to be amenable to its influences. *Znak* has had only five local clubs or organizations, *Pax* has sponsored over two hundred. Well supplied with funds, it has promoted cultural activities and lecture tours throughout the country, which have brought much larger audiences to *Pax* than to corresponding PZPR programs. *Pax* has succeeded in winning a larger audience for itself precisely because it has differed from the Communists in the content and approach of its written and spoken propaganda. In return for this success, it has demanded a large *de facto* share in the governance of Poland, and Piasecki himself is still believed to harbor grandiose personal ambitions.

Despite a measure of success, Piasecki can in no way really claim to speak on behalf of Polish catholicism in its millions and must therefore remain more of an auxiliary and less of a partner to the Communist rulers than he would like. Here the Church is clearly in Piasecki's way, for as Lucjan Blit has recently expressed it:

"The parish priest may not be the most forward-looking person in the world but he certainly is the accepted representative of the Church to all the believers in the village. His power, as the one who can refuse to christen a baby, marry a couple, and bury the dead in consecrated ground is so enormous that as long as he rules in his parish no party or government, and certainly no such 'heretics' as the *Pax* people are, can hope that the people will follow them and not him."[4]

After the October revolution Piasecki's *Pax* suffered something of a set-back. His group, led by Piasecki himself and Jerzy Hagmayer, had five deputies in the 1965 Sejm, even though Piasecki had demanded many more. The rich and extensive *Caritas* organization under Jan Frankowski split off. *Pax* also lost some previous tax exemptions. That he has not suffered any worse fate may well be the result of Piasecki's continuing Soviet connections. In 1956 Piasecki was a staunch supporter of Stalinist rule in Poland and openly, i.e., in his *Słowo Powszechne,* courted Soviet military intervention as an antidote to the liberalization which Gomułka was bringing about in Poland.

In this case, as well as subsequently, he has appeared to be more pro-Soviet and "radical" than the Polish Communist PZPR itself. Thus, after 1956 Piasecki sided with the most extreme Natolin die hards in favor of stepped up collectivization when the bulk of PZPR opinion, let alone general opinion in Poland, seemed solidly against this. In 1967 Piasecki's paper gleefully fanned the regime's so-called anti-Zionist campaign, adding "fuel to the fire" long after Gomułka had appealed for restraint. In 1968 Piasecki was instrumental in linking student demonstrations with the oldest theme in his ideology: anti-Semitism. *Słowo Powszechne* published the names of the parents of some of the student-demonstrators in Warsaw; the list emphasized names of Jews who were also ranking Party or Government functionaries. Piasecki called for a ruthless purge of "subversive elements" in Polish society and openly criticized Gomułka's leadership as "indecisive" and given to "half-measures." Although in 1956 he supported the Natolin group, in 1968 Piasecki seemed firmly ensconced behind General Moczar and the Partisans' bid for power. Having assailed Gomułka and sided with Moczar, Piasecki seemed to be staking his future upon the outcome of the Party's Fifth National Congress, which proved indecisive.

The downfall of Gomułka brought Piasecki a promotion in the form of membership in the Council of State in 1971, notwithstanding objections from the episcopate. Piasecki's fortunes in the wake of the December 1970 revolution depend in large measure on the ability of Edward Gierek to achieve a reconciliation with the Church. If the conflict between state and church could be eased, the regime would have less need for Piasecki's bogus catholicism. There have been indications in the several months preceding the fall of Gomułka that the episcopate was interested in promoting reconciliation. The Church hierarchy carefully refrained from injecting itself into such issues as the student unrest and the anti-Zionist campaign. Its reaction to the December 1970 strikes and riots was also cautiously reserved and circumspect. Gierek, for his part, has indicated strong interest in improving church-state relations. Thus, the 1970 revolution, like its 1956 predecessor, has begun on a note of hope in the coexistence of the Party and the Church.

Early in 1971 Cardinal Wyszyński condemned—retroactively—the attempt to rule Poland by repression, and he urged the Government to allow full freedom of religion, conscience and expression to the Polish people. The regime's response, this time, was conciliatory. A meeting between the Cardinal and Premier Piotr Jaroszewicz in Warsaw in March promoted a "thaw". The announcement in June that various church properties in the formerly German territories would be turned over to full-fledged ownership by the Polish episcopate evidenced the regime's interest in a *detente*. The Government was hopeful that at last Vatican recognition of Poland's Oder-Neisse frontier would be forthcoming. But misgivings on both sides continued. The Church was displeased with the enhancement of Boleslaw Piasecki; Cardinal Wyszyński publicly denounced the regime's restrictive population policies. And the regime resented Vatican "footdragging" on the recognition of People's Poland's frontiers. It still seemed unlikely that 1971, any more than 1956, would prove to be a really lasting turning point in State-Church relations.

The experience of Polish Communism since World War II is indicative of the remarkable strength and vitality of a people's religion as a bulwark against the penetration of an essentially alien political system. The Polish Party has had to associate itself with a "counterfeit Catholicism" in order to weaken the influence of genuine Catholicism. In suppressing virtually all secular opposition by the political parties and by associational interest groups, it only magnified the political power of institutionalized religion. It made Cardinal Wyszyński the *de facto* leader of the Polish opposition. Moreover, the Party's maladroit public confrontations with the Church, particularly in 1966, have suggested that it is the Cardinal and not the First Secretary of the Party who speaks for the great majority of the Polish people.

The Party has always insisted that it is prepared for a "live-and-let-live" policy toward the Church, notably expressed in the agreements of 1950 and 1956. Superficially, it professes to believe that Church-State conflicts in Poland spring mainly from the willful designs and reactionary prejudices of individual members of the Polish clergy, backed by "Vatican intrigue." What is really at issue, however, is the Party's effort to mould and control its social environment so thoroughly, and in a direction so profoundly hostile to the traditions of Polish Catholicism, as to make serious Church-State conflict endemic.

NOTES

1. On this subject see Albert Galter, *The Red Book of the Persecuted Church* (Dublin, 1957); Vladimir Gsovski (ed.), *Church and State Behind the Iron Curtain* (New York, 1955); George N. Shuster, *Religion Behind the Iron Curtain* (New York, 1954); see also Ronald C. Monticone, "The Catholic Church in Poland, 1945–1966," *The Polish Review*, vol. XI, no. 4, Autumn 1966, pp. 75–100, and Frank Dinka, "Church and State in Poland," *Review of Politics*, vol. 28, no. 4, October 1966, pp. 332–49.

2. See Delia and Ferdinand Kuhn, "The Cardinal Who 'Co-Exists'," *Harpers*, CCXV, November 1957, pp. 66–72.

3. See Lucjan Blit, *Gomulka's Poland* (London: Fabian International Bureau, 1959); and his *The Eastern Pretender, Boleslaw Piasecki, His Life and Times*, (London, 1965).

4. See *Ibid.*, p. 133. Cf. Robert Tobias, *Communist-Christian Encounter in East Europe* (Indianapolis, 1956); G. MacEoin, *The Communist War on Religion* (New York, 1951).

5

The Social and Economic Impact of Communist Rule

BEGINNING WITH THE land reform decree of 1944 by the so-called Polish Committee of National Liberation (PKWN), the Communists undertook to restructure the entire Polish economy and to subject it to direct, centralized, bureaucratic controls. In the years 1944–1946, over six million hectares of land* were redistributed by the regime from private holdings (most of them in the newly acquired German territories): to the peasants resettled from eastern Poland, to small owners, to the landless, and to state-operated farms. As a result of these reforms, over 90 percent of all the arable land still remained in private hands; most Polish farms, in fact, continued to be very small-size units, economically inefficient: many of them barely capable of sustaining the families settled upon the land. But the large private estates, the backbone of Poland's rural aristocracy, had been destroyed, and the regime carried out this reform without compensation to the former owners. An important social element opposed to the Communists was thus uprooted.

Land reform, however uneconomical in its results or arbitrary in its procedure, was a basically popular and in this sense a "safe" measure for the Communists to undertake. The mass of Polish peasantry clamored for a redistribution of the land long before World War II. Virtually all parties in Poland during the conflict were, in principle, pledged to reform.[1]

Simultaneously with the land reform program, the regime also began to take over industrial enterprises. A formal nationalization decree went into effect in 1946. It subjected all plants employing more than seventy persons to state ownership. Many of these larger enterprises

---

*1 hectare is about 2.5 acres.

were pre-war state monopolies (e.g., some 70 percent of the metallur-
gical enterprises were state-owned before 1939); some belonged to
owners who had been killed by the Nazis; some were left behind by
their German proprietors in the Oder-Neisse territories of the west.
The effects of expropriation began to be felt much more widely, however, between 1947 and 1950, when the regime proceeded to take over
most of the remaining private plants. In fact, by 1949, the private
sector accounted for less than 2 percent of Poland's industrial production. A substantial blow had been inflicted upon Poland's relatively
small urban middle class. The regime moved significantly closer to
total direct control of the economy.

Collectivization of the land, as the next step, would have given it the
power to manipulate and plan economic life on the model of Stalin's
Russia in the 1930s. Apart from ideological and political considerations, however, the Communists faced a monumental initial task in
bringing about some measure of recovery to a thoroughly war-shat-
tered economy. They were in no position to embark on a civil war
against the Polish peasant whose attachment to the land has been
traditionally tenacious. On the other hand, largely through Soviet
pressure and insistence, Poland was very quickly cut off from American
and western aid. Until the end of 1947, United States' funds, dis-
tributed through the United Nations Relief and Reconstruction Administration, supplied Poland with nearly 800 million dollars. But the
Soviet decision to reject the Marshall Plan brought an end to western
assistance and left Poland dependent upon the Soviet Union and upon
her own scant resources.

In the 1940s, the Russian economy was itself badly in need in
reconstruction. In fact, Soviet troops were "lifting" plants and equipment from Poland's western territories. The most substantial source
of capital immediately available to the Polish regime for development
schemes was agriculture, the country's basic resource. Beginning with
the Three Year Plan of 1947–1950, the Communists embarked upon
a consistent policy of exploiting the agricultural proprietors. Heavy
taxes and forced deliveries of products at low, state-set, prices were
combined with a lopsided channeling of investment funds and credit
for industrial and non-agricultural purposes to the several thousand
state farms carved out through the land reform of 1944–1946. The
regime thus attempted to coerce and coax peasant proprietors into
"voluntarily" becoming cooperative and state farm employees, by
economically "bleeding them dry."

Under the leadership of the State Planning Commission, created in
1949, the regime attempted direct central planning in virtually all the

branches of the economy. Specific and even minute performance targets, resource allocations, prices, wage schedules, and sundry details of operation were all being imposed from Warsaw down to the level of individual plants and enterprises throughout the country.

At the time of Stalin's death in 1953 the Polish economy was at its peak of bureaucratic regimentation and intensive industrialization. Economic isolation from the west and autarkic reliance on local resources were maximized. Forced, en masse collectivization of land was widely believed to be imminent. These trends were somewhat weakened in 1954 and 1955 following the death of Stalin. They were further weakened and undermined, if not wholly reversed, following the October 1956 "thaw," the return of Gomułka to power.[2]

Forced collectivization has been all but foresworn by the new Party leadership. Some state farm lands have been actually sold back to individual owners. Small-scale private enterprise has been given a significant respite from the liquidationist tendencies of the pre-1956 period. The sharp disparity between investments in industry and in agriculture has been appreciably narrowed. Economic contacts with non-Communist states have considerably increased. But the regime has not given up its centralized control of the economy, nor, as yet, the basic policy of sacrificing agriculture to industry, and, above all, consumption to capital investment.[3]

From a perspective of nearly 28 years we may gauge some of the major economic consequences of Communist rule. In many respects, the results which it has achieved have been genuinely spectacular. In 1945 Poland was akin to a vast battlefield piled with debris. The capital city of Warsaw was symbolic of the widespread damage caused by the war: 85 percent of the buildings lay in ruin. The ports of Gdynia, Gdańsk, and Szczecin were almost wholly wrecked. By various estimates nearly 40 percent of Poland's material national wealth had been destroyed; among her dead were Poland's leading intellectuals, scientists, teachers, and technicians. From this woeful state of destruction —relatively highest among World War II belligerents—she has made a remarkable recovery.

The economic achievements of the regime are circumstantially emphasized by the background of pre-war Poland. Unlike Czechoslovakia or East Germany, Poland before 1939 was a predominantly agricultural country. About 60 percent of the population drew its income from farming. In 1938 only one in eight employed persons worked in industry, which contributed less than 30 percent of the country's national income.

The pre-war Polish economy, particularly during the 1930s, was not only technologically backward but also dangerously stagnant. Between 1921 and 1931 the population rose by 5 million while industrial employment fluctuated between 700–800 thousand. In September 1938, Poland had 859,000 persons employed in industry; only 9000 more than in 1928! The rate of unemployment rose from 8 percent in 1928 to 13 percent in 1938, while population further expanded from 31 to 35 million during this decade. By some estimates, real per capita income in Poland fell by 16 percent between 1913 and 1938. These statistics were reflected in meager diets and inadequate housing, schooling, and medical care for millions of people.

In the late 1960s, the ratio of Polish population deriving its income from agriculture fell to about one-third. Poland's per capita industrial output rose to more than double the world average. In 1938 it was only 80 percent of that average. Since 1962 industry has contributed more than 50 percent of Poland's national income.

Among the more striking gross indices of industrialization, Polish output of coal rose from 38.1 million in 1937 to 125 million in 1967. Crude steel rose from 1.4 to 10.0 million tons; electric output from 4.0 to 50.0 billion Kw-h. Poland was now producing items never before represented in her economy, including automobiles, ships, and fishing vessels. Some 400,000 tons of sea-going craft launched in Polish shipyards in 1967 gave the country not only a new industry and a new export line but placed Poland eighth highest among the world's shipbuilders.[4] In terms of many economic indices, including the production of electric energy, coal, steel, cement, and zinc, Poland today ranks among the dozen industrial leaders of the world.

The rapid rate of industrialization has shifted Polish population to the towns, at a pace which is probably one of the fastest in Europe and the world. The number of towns of over 50,000 population has more than doubled in Poland since 1931. Where in 1931 some 4 million people out of a comparable population lived in towns, in 1966 8.4 million were urban dwellers. Thus, Poland today has all but reversed its prewar population structure as an agricultural and rural nation.

Poland's remarkable industrial expansion has been spurred not merely by the familiar ideological blueprint of communism, the accumulation of material resources for the transition to the higher stages of socialism and communism; or pressure from the Soviet Union for industrial-military goods as typically during the Korean War, or simply national pride in an age of technology. It has been rendered to some extent, at least, unavoidable by the rapid expansion of her population. Since the war, the Polish population growth, though somewhat diminished in the 1960s, has been among the highest in Europe. In the late 1940s and in the 1950s it was approximately twice as high as the average for the whole continent and much higher than in the prewar period. Thus, among the more remarkable demographic changes has been the emergence of Poland in the 50s and 60s as a predominantly young nation. Today more than 12 out of 32 million people in Poland are under the age of twenty, and virtually half of the total population is under the age of twenty-four.

The need to provide housing, schooling, and jobs for Poland's young people has made a policy of heavy capital investment at once mandatory and burdensome to the Polish economy. It has also brought the "population explosion" problem to the fore of public attention.

In the mid-and-late 1960s, Communist Poland suffered from serious unemployment both hidden and overt. By some estimates, 3.6 percent of the labor force (some 300,000 persons) was unemployed as of 1965, and some 18 per cent represented superfluous, unproductive employment.[5]

The relatively impressive results of Communist policies in the industrialization of Poland have not been matched in the expansion of agriculture. The effort to collectivize farming, by voluntary or quasi-voluntary means, has proved a failure both before 1956 and afterwards.[6] All the inducements, as well as threats and discriminatory practices applied against the peasantry, have proved unavailing. At the height of Polish Stalinism collectivization failed to absorb even a quarter of the arable land. In 1968 only about 13 percent of the land belonged to state-operated farms. As a consequence of the failure to collectivize the land, there has been no consolidation of Poland's traditional small holdings. And this in turn has impeded the progress of economically efficient, mechanized, modern production techniques. In fact, the division and subdivision of land has intensified since the reforms of 1944–46. Where in 1950, for example, about 25 percent of all farms were in the "dwarf" category (under 2 hectares), in 1960 the ratio increased to almost one-third. The number of farms with acreages of 2–3 hectares rose from 375.5 to 427 thousand; those between 3 and 5 hectares rose from 616.3 to 664.9 thousand. On the other end of the scale, the larger farms diminished in number. Those above 20 hectares declined from 39.9 to 34.5 thousand, those between 15 and 20 acres fell from 92.7 to 66.6 thousand. Moreover, the technical and economic problems of Poland's small farms were intensified by the heavy hand of the regime. Thus, the failure to make tractors and other agricultural machinery readily obtainable or purchasable by private cultivators has forced these to an extraordinary reliance upon the horse. In 1965 Poland possessed 15.1 horses per 100 hectares of arable land, the highest ratio in the world, and one which demands a highly uneconomical diversion of feed grains from cattle and other agricultural uses.*

In contrast to state operated farms, private holdings have been subjected to high taxes; starved of machinery, artificial fertilizers, and credits, and greatly disadvantaged in terms of total annual investment in agriculture. For example, the regime allocated more than 7 billion zlotys to the state farms in 1966. From both private and public sources, only 10.4 billion was invested in the private farms. Yet, the latter accounted for more than 80 percent of the arable land and produced nearly 90 percent of the country's agricultural output. Similar disparities have characterized state investments for many years before 1966, although they were even more drastic and inequitable before 1956.

Notwithstanding all these handicaps, private farming in Poland has managed to outperform state farms in the per hectare output of most grains, vegetables, potatoes, and, above all, in the production of livestock. In a country in which meat is relatively scarce and expensive, this has been a highly significant achievement. According to official data, private farms averaged 52.4 head of cattle per 100 hectares in 1965; state farms 48.2. Private farms averaged 74.2 pigs per 100 hectares; state farms 27.3. Private cultivators raised 16.0 sheep compared with state farms' 14.3 sheep per 100 hectares.

If the Polish experience has not yet proved communism a failure in the countryside, it has certainly not given it much encouragement. The output of Polish agriculture as a whole appears to have risen in spite of Communist policies, not because of them. Polish agriculture has kept ahead of the increases in population but hardly enough to afford a very substantial increase in living standards. Between 1950 and 1966 the population rose from 24.8 million to 31.7 million, i.e. by 25 percent. Agricultural production in 1966 was officially estimated at 160.0 percent of the average for 1950–52. By illustration, in the pre-war years 1934–38, crops were 112.7 percent of the 1950–52 average and animal products 96 percent.

Between 1949 and 1955, Polish agriculture experienced its least productive years. In 1955 its output was only 109.0 percent of the 1950–52 average or less than the increment in population. Between 1956–66 production increases have been on the average much higher. The progress of Polish agriculture during the years of Gomułka's leadership has probably provided the average Polish consumer with a

---

*A popular story circulating in Poland just before Gomułka's downfall was that when he had bad dreams, they were always about horses.

better diet, in terms of quality and quantity, than that of his prewar counterpart, particularly with respect to the consumption of meat, poultry, eggs, vegetables, and fruits. Recent data also show substantial per capita increases in the consumption of milk, dairy products, fish, sugar, and alcohol; modest increases in grain consumption and a decline in the intake of potatoes. Since 1949 the consumption of meat and animal fats has also risen. A general shift to diets with higher protein and vegetable content seems in progress.

Decreased mortality rates, particularly from tuberculosis, are also suggestive of more adequate levels of nutrition and personal care for the economically lowest strata of the population than was the case before 1939. To appreciate the proportions of this accomplishment, however, and its inadequacy in meeting the current demands of Polish consumers, we must appreciate its context: the dire poverty and widespread malnutrition among the prewar population.

Beyond its feats of industrialization, the command economy of Communist Poland has in fact approximated Galbraith's model of the affluent society in reverse. There has been relatively generous and effective spending on goods and services in the public sector of the economy; and this has had numerous beneficial consequences for the population. On the other hand, there has been inadequate provision of a variety of essential goods and services in the private sector with adverse impact on individual consumption and well-being.

The regime has provided the Polish people with greatly augmented resources in such fields as public health and medical care, social welfare, utilities, rents and transportation costs, culture, and education.

In 1938 there were 12,917 doctors in Poland averaging to only 3.7 per 10,000 persons. In 1968 Poland had 44,828 physicians, a ratio of 13.5 per each 10,000 of her population. The number of nurses increased from 6,674 to 92,163 so that in 1966 there were 26.5 nurses per each 10,000 people compared with only 1.9 in 1938. The number of dentists and pharmacists has more than tripled. The regime provided a total of 199,100 hospital beds in 1968, a ratio of 60.7 per 10,000. The corresponding figures in 1938 were 69,000 and 20.1.

An impressive network of clinics, rest homes, sanatoria, and hospitals has dispensed free medical care to the population. Drugs and medicines have been subsidized by the state for "out-patients" up to 70 percent of the costs.

These and similar measures augmenting public health services throughout the country, have, paradoxically, added to the population problem in Poland. Since the War infant mortality has declined from 140 deaths per 1,000 live births in 1938 to 41.4 in 1965. In the years

1935–39 the death rate was 14.1 per each 1,000 of the entire Polish population. In 1966 it was down to only 7.3. The average life expectancy in Poland has climbed from 48.2 years for men and 51.4 years for women in 1931–32 to 67.5 years and 72.9 years, respectively, in the period of 1963–65.

In 1966, the regime was paying old age, disability, and retirement pensions to 1,870,000 recipients, averaging 809 zlotys per month, i.e. somewhat above the minimum wage level. Old age pensions, at an average of 1,027 zlotys, were approximately one and one-half times the amount of the minimum monthly wage of 700 zlotys, and more than half of the average national wage in 1965: 1,873 zlotys after taxes.

Unfortunately, runaway inflation in the late 1960s and early 1970s nullified much of the value of Poland's social security system. One of the first measures of the Gierek regime in 1970 was to raise both the minimum wage and the basic old age pension by about one-third. Even so, the real value of these emoluments remained less than $35.00 a month. Admittedly, the Party has managed, since the very beginning of its rule in Poland, to keep certain family expenses all but negligible.

The costs of rents and utilities, as well as the costs of municipal and rail transportation historically have been maintained at very low levels by the Communist regime. Thus, typically, annual expenses of Polish families in 1966 on rents and utilities, heat and light, have been considerably less than ten percent of total family expenditure. The costs of transportation claimed less than five percent of annual family expenses. But housing itself has been extremely scarce.

Among publicly supplied goods and services which have been rendered at once more plentiful and less expensive to the average individual have been cultural attractions.

In 1938 pre-war Poland produced some 29 million books and monographs. In 1966 the figure rose to 98.8 million. The number of museums rose from 175 to 274; motion picture theaters from 807 to 3836; libraries attached to educational institutions increased their holdings from 7.6 million volumes in 1936 to 75 million in 1966. While data on pre-war Poland are not available in all of the cultural categories currently indexed by Polish statisticians, there is no doubt that since 1945 there has been an enormous increase in the exposure of the Polish people to sundry cultural media.

By every index, quantitative or qualitative, and with all due discount for the regime's implicit political purposes, much has been done in the fields of popular culture and science in Poland since 1945. Millions of inexpensive editions of native and foreign classics (including many English, American, and French as well as Russian works), scientific and reference guides have been made available to a rapidly growing reading public. In what is obviously a not inconsiderable achievement, the regime has expanded the number of public libraries from about 900 in 1947 to nearly 8200 in 1967; the number of volumes in their possession increased from 2.6 to 44.6 million during this period. There has also been a marked increase in widely available public exhibitions, lecture programs, and concerts.

Before the war Poland had ten radio stations and 1.1 million registered receivers. She now has twenty-two stations and nearly 6 million receivers in addition to some 3 million tv sets. Theatre and motion pictures have been greatly popularized. Where before the war Poland had some seventy permanent theatres, she had ninety-three of them in 1967. The repertoire has, particularly since the "thaw" of 1956, featured a great variety of plays by foreign as well as Polish writers. In 1961, for example, out of 499 Polish theatre premiers only thirty-eight featured works of Soviet authors; American playwrights accounted for twenty-seven performances. With heavy state subsidies and consequently low admission prices, the average annual theatre audience in Poland is estimated at about 18.9 million; it was only about 5.7 million with a higher over-all population before 1939. The Polish film industry has greatly expanded in sheer numbers of films, motion picture theatres, and film-goers.

Whereas Poland before the War possessed only one symphony orchestra—the Warsaw Philharmonic Society—there are now nineteen such ensembles in the country and 37 concert halls. Graphic art, which in the USSR has suffered so much from the deadening demands for socialist realism and condemnation of "bourgeois abstractionism," has flourished with fewer impediments in modern Poland. Polish architects, freed from the Stalin-era demands for stylistic orthodoxy, have charted new paths and brought Poland a measure of international acclaim.

Further important benefits to the population have been educational. Poland before the War suffered from fairly widespread illiteracy. At least 10 percent of school-age children did not attend any schools. Primary schools were too few and understaffed. Budgetary allotments for education before 1939 were notoriously meager. The higher levels of education—high schools, lycea, and universities—were relatively restricted in enrollment and catered predominantly to the needs of the economically well-to-do. During the Second World War the Polish educational system was subjected to a massive and unprecedented Nazi attempt at total extermination. Secondary school education was altogether forbidden to the Slav "untermenschen." Intellectuals became the favorite target of the firing squads and the concentration camps.

The Communists both revitalized and greatly expanded the educational system. Illustratively, where in 1937–38 there were 4,865,300 students in primary schools, the number rose to 5,527,100 in 1966–67. The number of teachers in these schools rose from 76.6 to 189.2 thousand. In 1938 83.3 thousand children attended kindergarten; 491.3 thousand did so in 1969. Advances in higher levels of education have been perhaps even more impressive. The number of institutions of higher learning rose from thirty-two to seventy-six. In 1967 there were 274.5 thousand full-time students in all the institutions of higher learning in Poland, where less than 49.5 thousand attended in 1938. Teacher training institutes increased from 74 to 178; students in them from 4,800 to nearly 40 thousand. The number of women in higher education rose dramatically from 14,083 in 1938 to 105,226 in 1967. Where in pre-war Poland there were 14 university-level students per each 1000 in the population, this ratio had gone up to 70 in 1967. There have also been great advances in the field of adult education. In mid-1960s more than half a million persons were being provided with some form of evening and part-time education, apart from regular degree programs. In 1966–67 trade schools enrolled 1.6 million persons compared to 207 thousand in 1937–38.

As a result of the rapid growth of Polish higher education, the number of trained personnel has greatly exceeded prewar levels. Where some 83,000 persons received university diplomas in the 1919–1939 period, the number rose to 344,000 from 1945 to 1963. As a consequence, about ninety percent of Polish intellectual workers today are trainees of People's Poland.

Free facilities and government stipends have played a major role in producing this large output of graduates. According to official estimates in 1966–67 some 75,000 students in higher education (some 30 percent of the total) were receiving financial aid from the state. Between 1951 and 1954, according to J. Wójcicka, about 78 percent of the students were thus aided. As late as 1957–1958, with a total enrollment of 162.8 thousand financial aid was given to 71.5 thousand. In 1937–38 stipends were being given to fewer than 10 percent of university students.

To be sure, all these advances have not been exacted without a price. Initially, at least, the regime obviously sacrificed quality of education for quantity in such a rapid expansion. In 1945 there were hardly enough qualified persons to staff the schools even at pre-1939 enrollment levels. The regime has also used the educational system as a vehicle for its ideological and political indoctrination programs, indeed as part of its larger pattern of cultural conquest. The rights of free expression, of criticism, and of traditional university autonomy have been severely curtailed, with the greatest repressions prevailing in the 1940s and 1950s, but still readily apparent in 1968 in consequence of recent student and faculty demonstrations.

In 1968, 1969, and 1970 the Polish regime summarily fired many of its distinguished senior academicians, either because of their Jewish origins or because of their political views. Many of these people, unable to continue their professional lives in Poland, sought exile in the United States, Denmark, Britain, Israel, and other countries. The process was reminiscent of the cultural purges going on simultaneously in Czechoslovakia, where scholars who had refused to endorse the Soviet invasion of 1968 were made to take on jobs as street cleaners, maintenance workers, railwaymen, and the like. It was a reminder of the price which the Party's dictatorship exacted for its relatively generous material investment in science and culture.[7]

If, nevertheless, the regime has managed to supply greatly increased and generally valuable social services to the people, it has not done nearly so well in providing the essentials of food, clothing, and goods of private consumption. It has withheld resources from the individual consumer diverting them to industrialization. Poland's housing situation is a dramatic illustration of the problem. To be sure, the regime has charged very low rents on existing buildings and has provided low-cost public utilities. It has also developed a high industrial potential for housing construction. Illustratively, Poland has increased her output of cement from 1.7 million tons in 1938 to 10 million tons in 1966. But the resources have not been committed to the construction of private dwellings.

According to official sources, the volume of dwellings constructed for purposes *other* than habitation has exceeded the latter in all but five years since 1950. The five years during which the balance was in favor of dwellings all belong to the Gomułka period (1957–1961) and in all of them, save 1958, industrial construction accounted for more than 45 percent of the total space built. In 1966, some 103,000 cu. ft. of new building space provided only 42,000 cu. ft. of dwelling space. Between 1950 and 1955 the total number of rooms available in Poland rose from 13,670,000 to 14,155,000, but this was not nearly enough to keep pace with the expansion of the population. There were then an estimated 1.94 persons per room in all of Poland compared with only 1.83 in 1950. In the urban areas the ratio went up from 1.54 to 1.77 per room.

In the ten year period between 1950 and 1960 urban overcrowding in Poland has changed only slightly. According to official data, the ratio of persons per room in 1960 was 1.53 to 1 in the cities and towns; it was 1.80 to 1 in the countryside. As late as 1966 the urban and rural occupancy ratios were still 1.41 and 1.66 persons per room, respectively. With all the augmented resources in steel, metals, machinery, chemicals, and fuels, People's Poland in 1968 provided about one private passenger car for each 100 inhabitants (323,424 cars in all) and only about one telephone for each sixty-five persons (506,600 altogether).

With respect to food and clothing, the regime has maintained a great gap between low, officially set wages and high, officially set prices. This has been done to minimize consumer pressure on scarce resources and to save capital for investment purposes. As a consequence, however, the average Polish consumer has suffered from long-standing privations.

Many products, readily purchasable in western Europe or the United States, for years have simply remained beyond the reach of most Poles. With all of the production advances since 1945, the great majority of Poles have not been able to enjoy the affluence of most Frenchmen, Germans, Britons or Italians even in terms of products which a less austere—or more efficient—Polish economy could supply to them more readily than the economies of, say, Britain or Italy.

The average salary of all those employed by the state in 1965 (8,-301,000 out of 8,427,000 classified as "employees") was 2119 zlotys. Actually 56.3 percent of these persons received salaries just at or below the level of 2000 zlotys. As is evident from the figures of Table 5:1, for all of these persons the purchase of many essential items could be accomplished only occasionally through prolonged savings. The minimum-wage earner who wished to buy himself the cheapest available suit out of his monthly salary would have to spend virtually all of it on the purchase. A pair of shoes could easily cost him more than half his monthly wage. Even for those with average incomes, the purchase of a suit would entail the expenditure of more than a third of their monthly salaries and possibly more than a full month's salary (2119 zlotys was only 1873 after taxes). Any person in the lowest one-third of the Polish salary scale had to spend between 10 and 20 percent of his monthly income on a single pair of children's shoes! Even in the top salary bracket, the purchase of a man's winter woolen coat—hardly a luxury in Poland's winter climate—entailed the spending of about one-third of a month's pay. For those in the lowest one-third, the purchase of a kilogram (2.2 pounds) of butter or ham would require the spending of 5–10 percent of the monthly wage. While the national

TABLE 5:1 Salary Structure and Some Representative Commodity Prices in September 1965.

Scale of monthly salary (in zlotys)	% of work force at the particu- lar salary level	Goods 1 Kg. = 2.2 lbs.	Prices in zlotys
700–800	3.2	Bread (1 Kg.)	3.50
		Flour (1 Kg.)	6.00
		Rice (1 Kg.)	8.00
801–900	2.4	Potatoes (1 Kg.)	1.40
		Sugar (1 Kg.)	12.00
		Chicken (1 Kg.)	47.00
901–1000	2.9	Eggs (1 doz.)	31.20
1001–1200	7.3	Ham (1 Kg.)	70.00
		Beef (1 Kg.)	36.00
1201–1500	14.7	Coffee (1 Kg.)	220.00
1501–2000	25.8	Tea (1 Kg.)	140.00
2001–2500	18.3	Butter (1 Kg.)	70.00
		Sausage (1 Kg.)	36.00–70.00
2501–3000	11.2		
3001–5000	12.5	Man's shirt	156.00
		Man's suit	660.00–1890.00
5001–	1.7	Man's shoes	220.00–450.00
5001–	1.7	Women's shoes	180.00
		Baby shoes	136.00
		Women's stockings	33.00–51.00
		Man's winter coat	700.00–1540.00
		Women's winter coat (100% wool)	1360.00
		Man's watch	700.00
		Man's bicycle	992.00
		Motorcycle	8000.00
		Radio	700.00
		Television set	7000.00
		Refrigerator	3000.00–6000.00
		Automobile (Polish Syrena)	72000.00
		Camera	1200.00
		Sewing machine	2615.00
		Washing machine	2050.00
		Clothes closet- cabinet (large, 3-door)	2100.00
		Upholstered couch	2150.00

income since 1950 has more than doubled, the rise in individual incomes has been only about one-third. Polish wages continue among the lowest in Europe in terms of their real purchasing power.

The great and continuing disparity between wages and prices, and the dearth of consumer goods, have been part of the impact of Communist rule on Poland. It was this gap between spiraling official production figures and the deadly dreariness of every day lives which made the Poznań workers say that they were tired of "working for the future." They demanded more for the present, and the bulk of their demands still remains to be met.

The Gomulka regime did not reverse the one-sided pattern of public investment which characterized pre-1956 Communist Poland. Under the 1960–1965 5-year plan the distribution of investment was set at 83.8 percent to the capital goods sector; 16.2 percent to consumer goods. In the "Stalinist" year of 1953 the ratios were remarkably similar: 87 to 13 percent. Stagnant wage levels and an endemic inflation set the stage for the revolt against Gomulka in December 1970. The decree raising food prices some 20 percent on December 13th was the proverbial straw which broke the camel's back.

High prices and the dearth of consumer goods have been accompanied by other serious problems. Centralized planning and the employment of a vast army of bureaucratic functionaries for its execution have augmented the hardships in the everyday lives of the Polish people. The quantity and quality of goods available to the Polish housewife have been determined not by market demand but by the political, bureaucratic apparatus. This has frequently resulted in the manufacture and distribution of products not really wanted by consumers and also in a lack or undersupply of other items eagerly sought by the shopping public. In the pre-1956 period, considerations of style, variety, and color in the manufacture of clothes and household goods were virtually brushed aside by the planners in favor of standardized, less costly, less complex types of products—often shoddy in workmanship and unappealing in appearance. Where mistakes were made in the planners' calculations, people would sometimes queue for hours before Government-run stores only to come back home emptyhanded. In the early fifties, for example, hairpins became extremely scarce one year simply because the planners had forgotten to make provision for their manufacture.

Similiar problems have developed in the servicing of consumers. Unconcerned with profits, or with competition, the bureaucratic officialdom operating the wholesale and retail trade outlets has not been particularly anxious to please. The amenities and the efficiency associated with the motto is not readily applicable in Poland. Customer good will has meant little to economic managers and employees whose jobs and promotions have depended on fulfilling norms set at the top, not in catering to the "whims" of consumer demand.

Bureaucratic red tape has been coupled with corruption. In many instances Government distributors have sought to make personal profit out of shortages of goods. In most cases, of course, black market selling and outright thefts by state employees have not been publicized in the Government press. But there have been telling exceptions. In August, 1964, eighteen PZPR officials were brought to trial in Warsaw in connection with the discovery of a large-scale black market and thefts of meat. To most Poles it seemed like the visible tip of an immense iceberg.

An effort to decentralize planning, allow more consumer choice, and give more flexibility to local economic units, such as factories, farms, and stores, had been much discussed but never effectively implemented under the Gomułka regime.[8] The Party has been obviously reluctant to give up its directing role in the economy. It has been concerned with the political and economic consequences of allowing the free play of supply and demand. To accommodate the preferences of consumers would inevitably lead to a drastic cutback in the Party's ambitious industrialization program. It could also undermine the position of state-owned enterprises in the Polish economy as these might not be able to keep pace with the private and cooperative sectors. It might also mean the acceptance of some unemployment in order to rationalize production; this, however, the Party has found politically unpalatable, even at the cost of present relative labor inefficiency and featherbedding.

In reviewing the primarily economic aspects of Communist rule in Poland since 1945, one cannot fail to be impressed by its central paradox. The regime's greatest successes and most abysmal failures have been economic. Judged against the background of prewar Poland and the deprivations of the war itself, striking progress has been made in the public sectors of the economy—not simply in industry but in a broad category of public utilities and facilities like schools, hospitals, clinics, libraries, playgrounds, theaters, concert halls, and the like.

However, the effort required to achieve all of these advances has been such as to hold back the living standards of the Polish people in terms of the privately consumed, indispensable essentials: food, clothing, and shelter. By the Party's own admission, the real wages of Polish workers actually declined between 1949 and 1955.

Mounting production figures—unrelated or even inversely related to consumption—could satisfy little more than a craving for national prestige. The undeniable benefits and increased opportunities created for the people by an expansion of public services and facilities could hardly seem more than marginal to those unable to satisy essential needs for clothes, shoes, an appealing diet and adequate housing. For many workers and state employees in the early 1950s it became literally *necessary* to steal in order to survive and the practice continues.

As S. L. Schneiderman wrote in his *Warsaw Heresy* of 1959: "Theft is an economic necessity in Poland because the wage scale is still miserable. The average salary of a worker . . . is between 1000 and 1200 zlotys a month. Comparably, the price of a pair of shoes is 300–400 zlotys, and a cheap suit of clothes costs 1500–2000 zlotys. To make ends meet, workers work two shifts and take on additional Sunday jobs because the normal work week in Poland is still a full six days."

Since 1959 the wage and price levels cited by Schneiderman have gone up but the basic relationships between them have not really changed much. Whatever other attainment the regime may have secured, its inability to eliminate theft as a widespread supplement to income has been one of its great moral as well as economic disasters.

The Gomułka regime by no means reversed the basic economic pattern set before 1956, and, like all regimes everywhere, it was caught in the spiral of rising popular expectations. The Polish people were not satisfied to know that "under socialism" they were better off in some respects, at least, than their fathers and grandfathers had been in the 1930s. Their eyes have been upon the contemporary achievements of Western nations.

In addition to material, "pocket-book" impact, Communist rule in Poland has had other significant social consequences. The regime has created a virtually new, socio-economic and managerial elite larger and more broadly based than its pre-World War II predecessor. Peasants, workers and women have gained entry into this elite through the expanded educational system at a much higher rate than was the case before 1939.

The largest single group of university students before World War II was recruited from the children of middle-class white collar workers and those with trade and professional family backgrounds. This group constituted 57.5 percent of the students in 1937–38. Other well-to-do groups, including those drawn from the landed aristocracy and upper middle-class background amounted to 25.6 percent. Students of working class origin accounted for only about 9 percent and peasants 8 percent.[10]

According to data compiled by Janina Wójcicka, students of working class backgrounds constituted 34.8 percent of university enrollments in the 1954–55 period and those of peasant background 24.9 percent. In 1963–64, according to Polish official data, among those receiving regular daytime instruction in the institutions of higher learning the ratio of workers was 26.3 percent; peasant backgrounds accounted for 18 percent. The white-collar intelligentsia still dominated with 49.7 percent of enrollments; children of tradesmen and craftsmen accounted for 4.8 percent and unspecified "others" only 1.2. The balance in favor of persons of working class and peasant origins was somewhat higher among those engaged in part-time, evening, and correspondence study.

In 1966–67 among nine types of institutions—universities, university-level schools of technology, agriculture, economics, education, medicine, physical training, art, and theology—the proportion of white collar elements constituted a plurality in all but one and a majority in five of these. But those of worker and peasant backgrounds accounted for more than 40 percent of the students in six of the nine branches of higher education and averaged 43.5 percent of the total enrollment.

Obviously, an annual influx of between 40 and 55 percent of worker-peasant elements, over a period of some twenty-odd years, has modified the character of Poland's white collar intelligentsia. It has become a different social compound from its prewar counterpart. On the other hand, judging by the recent changes in the compositions of Party organs, the Government, and various units of administration, the political role of this new intelligentsia is being constantly enhanced. It remains to be seen whether the consequences of this enhancement will ultimately redound to the benefit of the regime. Among the more disquieting statistics of the postwar period, from the Communist point of view, is the fact that of all the branches of higher education, the proletarian, worker-peasant elements are by far most preponderant in theology (62.3 percent in 1966–67)!

Another significant social consequence of communist rule has been a narrowing down of income differences among people. The Polish wage structure has tended to narrow the gap between the purchasing power of the "top" and "bottom" of the social pyramid.

The salaries of the highest government officials, scientists, writers, artists, and the like have been maintained markedly within a less than 10 to 1 ratio as compared with lowest level unskilled laborers and those receiving the minimum wage. In 1965 with the average wage at 2119 zlotys, nearly 60 percent of all employees ranged between 1200 and 2500 zlotys; 83.5 percent ranged between 1200 and 5000. Those earning between 700–800 zlotys represented only about 6 percent of the work force. There was also a remarkable balance between wages paid to those doing manual and non-manual work. Among the highest paid employees, manual workers receiving between 3000 and 5000 zlotys accounted for 11.2 percent of the labor force, while non-manual workers in that income category accounted for 14.7 percent. Even in the highest bracket of over 5000 zlotys shared by only 1.7 percent of all Polish employees, 1 percent represented manual workers, mainly miners and skilled technicians, as against 2.9 percent of non-manual employees.

But these achievements, too, have had their seamy side. In the eyes of many people, the new elite has assumed the role of the exploiter class, fleecing and oppressing the workers and other poor people no less despicably and even more despotically than its capitalist predecessors. Moreover, progress toward equality, in strictly material terms, has not been all that it seems or that it might be. People's Poland has managed to reduce the prewar gap between a nobility that included the wealthiest landholder in all of Europe, Count Maurycy Zamoyski, and the many people who openly begged in the streets. Yet it continues to be acutely embarrassed—in view of its Marxist aspirations to egalitarianism—by the perquisites of its leading bureaucrats and assorted profiteers with official connections. Unlike the great masses of Poland's workers and peasants, a relatively small elite enjoys the luxuries of private automobiles, villas, foreign vacations, plentiful food, and custom-made clothes. These people, in the words of recent critics, constitute the privileged stratum of a centralized party bureaucracy. Milovan Djilas called them the New Class. For these people, widespread poverty is desirable, not as a temporary sacrifice for the ultimate achievement of a classless paradise, but as a means of keeping the masses docile and thus enabling the New Class to perpetuate more readily its own power.

After twenty-five years of Communist rule, all its collectivist and egalitarian tendencies notwithstanding, Poland still retains a significant residue of small-scale private enterprise. The Polish entrepreneur of the 60s is more often than not a man who operates his own workshop, his own taxi or his own newspaper stand. In 1966 there were over 147 thousand individual workshops with about 280 thousand operators; of these 149 thousand were owners and 76 thousand were employees. Since 1955 there has been a steady increase in private building firms which, on a small scale, fill the gap between public demand for housing and government supply of it. In 1955 there were 5.9 thousand private building firms with 5979 owners and 3.7 thousand employees. In 1966 there were 34.9 thousand firms; 35 thousand owners and 25.1 thousand employees. One form of ownership which in Poland has combined private and collective effort has been cooperative building of private dwellings—so nortoriously lacking. Houses are constructed from the pooled savings of individuals and state subsidies. The cooperatives assume ownership through long-term mortages. Cooperative and individual construction jointly has accounted for about 40 percent of all dwellings built in Poland since 1956.

The survival and expansion of various forms of privately owned and managed businesses suggests that the regime has by no means wholly extinguished the Polish middle class, either rural or urban. Even in the era of Polish Stalinism, private establishments of industrial, handicraft, or service character managed to maintain their existence. These establishments included all sorts of repair shops, blacksmiths, dry cleaners, photographers, hairdressers, barbers, and also small-scale manufacturers of various products. In 1950, these workshops had a personnel of about 159 thousand persons, of whom 106 thousand were proprietors and members of their families. Employees and apprentices accounted for the remaining 73 thousand.

Between 1950 and 1953 the regime reduced the number of private workshops to less than 83 thousand and the personnel to about 124 thousand; of these persons only 47 thousand were actually salaried employees of private enterprise. Beginning with 1954, however, there has been an upturn in all the indices of private crafts and industry. 1956–57 produced the largest annual increase in the number and size of private establishments, and it has been followed by a more gradual and unspectacular progress to current figures.[12]

Among private trade and catering establishments the trend has been somewhat less favorable to individual ownership since 1950, but they still have a significant and relatively stable share of economic activity. In 1966, there were some 22 thousand private retail stores in Poland compared with about 100 thousand maintained by the state, and 180 thousand by various cooperatives. Actually, an undisclosed number of state stores, according to official sources were being "operated by private retailers through special contracts" with the state. Out of some 12 thousand restaurants in Poland, 900 were privately owned in 1966. Out of about 59 thousand "mobile selling units"—vendors, carts, newspaper stands, etc.,—more than 8 thousand were privately operated.*

Twenty-five years of Communist rule—in its Polish variety—have produced enormous economic and social changes. But they have not

---

*Early in 1971, Party leader Gierek announced plans to increase taxes on private businesses by 10 to 15 percent to finance increased pensions and family subsidies.

changed the society and the economy quite as drastically as Communist rule had changed it in Russia and in most of the other East European nations during a comparable period.

The effects of Communist achievements, such as they are, on the stability and future prospects of Communist rule are open to doubt. To what extent is the Communists' record actually favorably perceived by the population? Is it outbalanced by the memories of their Soviet-backed seizure of power? Is it outweighed by their other, less popular or successful policies?

The technical, cultural, scientific, bureaucratic, and increasingly political leadership of the new Poland has been trained, in its great majority, after 1945. More of its members have come from the lower, worker-peasant, strata of the population than ever before. The traditional links of the pre-war Polish intelligentsia to the nobility and to the affluent middle classes have been substantially severed. But if People's Poland today is largely dominated by a "People's Intelligentsia," the political consequences of this fact are a matter of speculation. Are these new intellectuals and leaders likely to support the rule of the Party out of gratitude or as a vested interest of their own? We cannot forget that the underlying values, attitudes, and traditions of the Polish worker and peasant have not been hospitable either to the communist creed or to its Russian sponsors and backers.

The workers' gains in terms of social mobility and publicly provided cultural and social services have been offset by losses in other areas, particularly in collective bargaining, the exploitation of labor, and the maintenance of labor discipline.

Transformed into docile Party instruments, the unions during the 1950s did not prevent unusual and excessive exploitation of labor or cuts in real wages which the regime undertook in order to reach its industrial goals.[13]

One may wonder whether, as in the case of the USSR, the material and cultural advances recorded under Communist rule could not have been realized—and perhaps exceeded—without it; whether the costs in freedom and in the sufferings of persecuted opponents have not been excessive.

Can the Communists eventually convert social and economic accomplishments into popular acceptance of the legitimacy of their rule, as suggested by S. M. Lipset? So far, the Party has implemented one Three-Year Economic Reconstruction Plan (1947–1949); a Six-Year Plan for the Construction of Socialism (1950–1955) and two Five-Year Economic Development Plans (1956–1960, and 1961–1965). The PZPR's long range program—publicized in 1964—called for the completion of the "construction of socialism" and the "advanced building of Communism" in Poland by 1980. In the latter phase, under the slogan "from each according to his ability to each according to his needs", the quintessence of a benevolent and opulent welfare state program would presumably be reached—but without those coercive and punitive aspects of governmental control which the Marxist theory associates with the very notion of the "State." The plan called for a roughly three-fold increase in Poland's present national income and a four-fold growth in industrial output by 1980. Poland was to produce 24 million tons of steel; 160 million tons of coal and 175 million Kwh of electric energy. The plan would give Poland a higher per capita production of most industrial products than that heretofore reached by any West European country, and in some cases even higher than that of the United States currently. By 1980 the urban population of Poland was to constitute between 60 and 70 percent of the total.

The December upheaval deflected the PZPR from its millenarian visions of industrialization. The Polish consumer evidenced a critical breaking point, one that the Party could not afford to ignore. The new Five Year Plan for 1971–75 which Gierek presented to the Sixth Party Congress indicated a trend toward "consumerism" more on the model of Kadar or Tito than of Stalin or even Gomułka.

NOTES

1. Cf. Witold Staniewicz, "The Agrarian Problem in Poland Between the Two World Wars," *Slavic and East European Review*, vol. 43, winter 1964, pp. 23–33; and also A. A. Rozental, "The Land of the Peasant," *Survey*, No. 25, July-September 1958, pp. 17–22; and Stanisław Skrzypek, "Agricultural Policies in Poland," *Journal of Central European Affairs*, XVI, April 1956, pp. 45–70.

2. Thad Paul Alton, *Polish Postwar Economy* (New York, 1955); Bolesław Bierut, *The Six Year Plan of Economic Development and Building the Foundations of Socialism in Poland* (Warsaw, 1950); W. J. Stankiewicz and J. M. Montias, *Institutional Changes in the Postwar Economy of Poland,* (New York, 1955); Oskar Lange, *Some Problems Relating to the Polish Road to Socialism* (Warsaw, 1957).

3. See two articles by John M. Montias, "Unbinding the Polish Economy," *Foreign Affairs*, XXXV, April 1957, pp. 470–484; "The Polish 'Economic Model'," *Problems of Communism*, IX, No. 2, March-April 1960, pp. 16–24.

4. For the most recent figures see *Rocznik Statystyczny 1967*, Główny Urzad Statystyczny, Warsaw, September 1967.

5. See Bogdan Mieczkowski, "Bezrobocie w systemie komunistycznym," *Kultura* (Paris) no. 11/254, November 1968, pp. 92–100.

6. For a thorough survey see Andrzej Korboński, *Politics of Socialist Agriculture in Poland: 1945–1960* (New York, 1965).

7. Cf. N. Apanasiewicz, *Educational Systems in Poland*, Washington: Department of Health, Education and Welfare, 1959; N. Buhler and S. Żukowski, *Discrimination in Education in the People's Democracies* (New York: Mid-European Studies Center, 1955); Mid-European Research Center, *The Sovietization of Culture in Poland* (Paris, 1953). On this relatively generous material endowment of education and culture as characteristic of all Communist systems, see A. J. Groth and L. L. Wade, "Educational Policy Outcomes in Communist, Democratic and Autocratic Political Systems" APSA paper, September 1970, and more generally still, A. J. Groth, *Comparative Politics: A Distributive Approach* (New York, 1971). It is worth noting that the high level of "objective" cultural-educational spending in Poland did not forestall criticism of the Gomułka regime that it was not doing enough and that it ought to be doing more in these areas.

8. See Leon Smoliński, "Economics and Politics: Reforms in Poland," *Problems of Communism*, July-August 1966, vol. XV, no. 4, pp. 8–13.

9. *Op cit.*, p. 121–22.

10. Cf. Leopold Labedz, "Sociology and Social Change," *Survey*, no. 60, July 1966, pp. 18–39

11. See Jan Drewnowski "Socjalizm w Polsce" *Kultura* (Paris) No. 9/276, September 1970, pp. 25–39, on Poland's bureaucracy as a new ruling class, stressing the role of theft and corruption among its crucial perquisites.

12. See Jan Przybyła, "Private Enterprise in Poland Under Gomułka," *Slavic Review*, XVII, no. 3, October 1958, pp. 316—331. Cf. Drewnowski, *op. cit.* on private enterprise as a valuable source of "spoils" for the party bureaucracy.

13. See François Fejto, "Trade Unionism in East Europe: The Conflict Between Working Class Ties and the Single Party," *International Affairs*, XXXIII, October 1957, pp. 427–441.

6

Foreign Policy

FOREIGN POLICY OCCUPIES a special place in the framework of Communist rule in Poland. Its domestic role is no less significant than the external.

The active and passive acceptance of the Party's rule is based to a large extent on the widespread belief—encouraged by the Party—that the Soviet Union would tolerate only a Communist government on its Polish doorstep. The Hungarian experience of 1956 has been widely regarded as indicative not only of what the Russians might do if "pushed too far" but also of the disinterest of the West. To many East Europeans, Poles among them, 1956 indicated Western unwillingness to risk a world war with Russia in behalf of liberating the so-called satellites.

The Russian invasion of Czechoslovakia in August 1968 (with auxiliary participation by Poland, East Germany, Hungary, and Bulgaria) was a confirmation of the Soviet resolve to resist unwelcome changes in Eastern Europe, by force, if necessary. In November 1968, the leader of the Soviet Communist Party, Leonid Brezhnev, used the forum of the Polish Party's Fifth National Congress in Warsaw to reaffirm his so-called Brezhnev Doctrine. Soviet armed forces would intervene to prevent the overthrow of "socialist" regimes in Eastern Europe, he asserted. Since Brezhnev was, no doubt deliberately, vague about the geographic limits of his doctrine, even the Yugoslavs and the Albanians stirred uneasily. Few Poles doubted that the Russians would apply it toward them. And, indeed, during the December 1970 riots which culminated in Gomułka's resignation, Soviet armored units were reported ready for an attack against Poland from their bases in East Germany and the USSR; some were, of course, stationed within the Polish frontiers.

118

Nevertheless, the Party has always sought to bolster this largely negative position of submitting to superior Soviet force with the more positive "German argument." It has historically resorted to a refurbished version of the nationalist theory of Dmowski: Russian and Polish interests coincide against those of Germany. Assessing the situation in Western Europe, the Party takes the view that "realistically" only the countervailing power of the USSR can stem the sooner or later unavoidable German attempt at *revanche*, the consequent loss of the Western territories by Poland, and even a new subjugation by Germany.

The increasing momentum of reconciliation with West Germany since 1968, culminating in the recognition of Poland's Oder-Neisse frontier by the Government of Chancellor Willy Brandt, has weakened this argument somewhat. But the PZPR position still is that whatever Germans may promise or agree to do, now or ever, only Soviet backing for Poland can truly secure.

Without a widespread belief among Poles that close links with the Russians are not merely desirable but simply unavoidable, the Party certainly could not peacefully maintain its preponderant power. If appeasement of Moscow were no longer really *necessary,* acquiescence in the Party's autocratic rule would also forefeit its "essential" and "inevitable" character.

Yet, the pressures on the Communists to maintain close contact with the Soviets have always been opposed by certain countervailing pressures from within. Subservience to the Russians is a bitter pill for most Poles. The course of maximizing the Party's popular appeal cannot possibly lie in that direction. Also, there are some inevitable and natural strivings within the Party's own ranks to independence and autonomy, particularly as the new home-grown generation of Party leaders takes over from the aging Muscovites. Alliance with the Soviet Union may be essential to the viability of any Polish-Communist regime. But for Communism to appear Polish—not Russian—in the eyes of the Polish people, a degree of uniqueness and independence are required in its foreign as well as domestic policies.

Under Bierut, Poland was essentially but an amplifier or "transmission belt" of Soviet foreign policy positions. In 1947 she refused to participate in the Marshall Plan, following the lead given by the Soviet Foreign Minister Molotov. Until the inauguration of Gomułka's new course she supported Soviet policies in the United Nations, by voice and vote, without even minor "deviations." American imperialism along with German militarism were the objects of continual, strident Polish denunciations. Assistance given by Polish diplomatic representatives to Soviet espionage and propaganda in the United States and other western countries led to the closing down of numerous Polish diplomatic posts abroad.

These developments were not really unwelcome to Poland's Stalinist masters. The Bierut-Berman regime attempted to isolate Poland from "corrosive" western influences. It opposed "bourgeois cosmopolitanism," as all efforts at international understanding and cooperation were dubbed by Communists in the heyday of Stalinism. Instead, it proposed the ideal of "proletarian internationalism," which in practice involved little more than support of Soviet international policies in the name of the alleged common interest of the working classes of all countries. After 1948, the regime joined in the Soviet propaganda, diplomatic, and economic campaign against Tito. Tito's espousal of an independent course at home and abroad earned him the unqualified Polish condemnation as a renegade, a stooge of American imperialism and even a fascist. Gomułka, who had closely identified with Tito in advocating a relatively independent Communist course for Poland and who objected to servile imitations of the Soviet example was, of course, purged.

Poland's international position was characterized by increasing dependence on the Russians. Economically, this dependence followed from the rejection of the Marshall Plan and the general isolation and estrangement from the West. In the process, Russia became the principal source of Polish capital equipment and credits, which she supplied in return for deliveries of Polish raw materials, at below world-market prices, primarily coal.[1] In 1949, the Soviets attempted to institutionalize this dependence of their "satellites" by the establishment of the so-called Council of Mutual Economic Assistance (COMECON) with the initial, avowed purpose of coordinating trade among the East European economies and with non-Communist nations. Gradually, the purposes of this organization have been extended to include multilateral development planning, specialization and coordination of economic functions among the several Communist states, and the promotion of economic growth.[2]

Diplomatically and militarily, Poland's links to Russia were sanctioned by a 1945 Treaty of Friendship and Mutual Assistance and reinforced by similar links to the several East European Communist nations. The network of bilateral treaties was replaced by the Warsaw Treaty in 1955, linking Poland with Russia, East Germany, Czechoslovakia, Rumania, Hungary, and Bulgaria in a joint defense system. The Warsaw Pact was signed on May 14, 1955, barely two months after the entry of West Germany into NATO.[3]

The Pact has been traditionally pictured by the Soviet and Polish regimes as a response to the creation of an aggressive military alliance, instigated by Americans and revanchist Germans, and directed against them. Actually, it has been used to provide legal cover for the continued maintenance of Soviet troops in such countries as East Germany, Poland, Hungary, and Rumania. In 1956 the Russians used the Pact as a justification for their intervention in the Hungarian Revolution, a position which, significantly, Poland has never publicly endorsed. In 1958 all Soviet forces were finally withdrawn from Rumania but not from the other states. As of 1972 at least two Soviet divisions still remain stationed in Poland.

The Commander-in-Chief of the Warsaw Pact forces is invariably a Soviet officer, since 1967 Marshal Ivan I. Yakubovsky. Each participant nation's Minister of Defense is considered ex-officio Deputy Commander-in-Chief of the Warsaw Pact forces, but joint planning is a function of the Soviet general staff.

Poland—along with other East European states—has helped to develop a protective air-defense system as a shield for the Soviet Union. The Soviets have supplied Polish forces with a variety of military equipment—some of it obsolete and phased out of Soviet programs— including missiles. Neither nuclear nor offensive strategic weapons such as heavy bombers or IRBMS have been supplied.

The Polish contribution to the Warsaw Pact is, nevertheless, second only to that of the USSR. The Poles provide the largest land army, some 300,000 men, in addition to a small Baltic fleet manned by about 20,000 sailors, and an air force of about 800 aircraft. Poland's military spending in terms of her Gross National Product is third highest of the Warsaw Pact powers (5.3 percent), behind the Soviet Union (8.9 percent) and Czechoslovakia (5.7 percent).

Soviet military organs currently refer to Poland—along with East Germany and Czechoslovakia—as the first strategic echelon of the Warsaw Pact, an area of apparently greater strategic significance to the Soviet Union than Hungary, Rumania, or Bulgaria. In recent years Poland has been one of the staunchest backers of the USSR in the Pact's councils, principally in opposition to the Rumanians, who have questioned the continued usefulness of the Pact and objected to its domination by the Russians. Not until the Berlin crisis of 1961, however, have the Polish forces participated with Soviet, Czechoslovak, and East German troops in joint military exercises.

The reliability of the Polish army has been something of a problem for the Soviets. In the 1940s and early 1950s it clearly suffered from a dearth of politically dependable and technically competent leaders. Until 1956 there were approximately seventeen thousand Soviet offic-

ers in the Polish Army: fully half of the officers' corps. Many, though
by no means all, have been weeded out after 1956. In 1963, 70 percent
of all Polish officers were reported to be PZPR members, but this in
itself was no certain index of their trustworthiness from the Soviet
point of view. It appears that the USSR still sees Warsaw Pact forces
as a potential auxiliary to its own troops, but the alliance has been
affected by the growing political ferment in Eastern Europe, most
recently in Czechoslovakia.

The years 1968–1971 have seen a very significant realignment in
Poland's foreign policy. West Germany has evolved from the role of
Poland's chief external enemy to that of a potentially friendly neighbor. Simultaneously, in the last years of the Gomułka regime Poland
grew more and more subservient to the Soviet Union. Both developments reversed Polish policies characteristic of the period of Gomułka's relative "liberalism."

Partly in response to the new initiatives of Chancellor Willy Brandt,
partly in response to the increasing Soviet interest in a rapproachment
with West Germany, Warsaw's mood of intransigence and suspicion
dissipated. In May 1969, Gomułka publicly offered to negotiate a separate treaty with West Germany on the frontier issue, provided that
Bonn recognized the independence and territorial integrity of East
Germany and adhered to the Nuclear Nonproliferation Treaty. In
June, Klaus Schutz, the Mayor of West Berlin, was invited to visit the
Polish trade fair in Poznań. He was the highest ranking West German
official to visit Poland since World War II. The Polish leadership and
the Party press were at last beginning to take notice of some "healthy
and positive" signs of reconciliation in West Germany. In February
1970 substantial negotiations between Warsaw and Bonn got under
way, continuing through most of the year. A trade pact was agreed
upon in June; consular relations in July; Polish-German agreement on
the key Oder-Neisse issue was unofficially reported as early as June; in
August, the West German Government emphasized its good will toward Poland by cutting off public support to militant German refugee
organizations in West Berlin still intransigent in their demands for the
return of the Oder-Neisse lands.

Polish-German frontier agreement was dramatically formalized in
the Treaty of December 7, 1970, when Chancellor Brandt journeyed
to meet Gomułka in Warsaw. Here, for what has been aptly described
as an electrifying moment, Brandt knelt before the monument to the
Jewish martyrs of the Warsaw Ghetto, as if in official atonement.

Apart from the new mood of Polish - German reconciliation, however, many crucial questions of Poland's future course remained unan-

swered in the wake of the Treaty of December 7, 1970. As of early 1971, both the agreement with Poland and a similar Mutual Security Treaty between the Soviet Union and West Germany (signed August 8, 1970) had not yet been submitted to the West German Parliament for ratification by the Brandt Government. West German opposition to these treaties was substantial. The relationship between West and East Germany, the fate of West Berlin, and still larger issues of all-European security and disarmament remained to be settled. The impact of the transition from Gomułka to Gierek in Poland was also an unknown element.* Conceivably, a start had been made toward a wholly new era in Polish- West German relations. If that were the case, Poland's relations with East Germany would likely change, too. Increased trade and contacts with West Germany would present new opportunities for the Poles; but they could also lead to new tensions with the Soviets, as the cases of Czechoslovakia and Rumania seemed to indicate. This may be true even if, as is likely, it was Soviet "encouragement" which helped Gomułka change his attitude toward West Germany.

Above all, however, the domestic impact of the new relationship was likely to be important. Heretofore, the Party had relied on the stereotype of West German "revanchism" and "imperialism" to justify its particular version of the garrison state. What effective substitutes could it find for the traditional German enemy? Could it really dispense with such a device under the more pragmatic, hopefully more de-ideologized and liberal leadership of Edward Gierek? If reconciliation with West Germany was but a first step to a reconciliation with Western Europe, with NATO, and with the Common Market, would this not weaken the rationale of Communist rule in Poland?

Kremlin designs and anxieties notwithstanding, the future of both COMECON and the Warsaw Pact in the early 1970s appeared very much in doubt. To this change in the international situation of East-Central Europe, Gomułka's Poland historically had made some significant contributions. The Poles were the first to combine, successfully, a role of outward alliance and friendship with the USSR on the one hand, with a significant measure of independence on the other. To be sure, since 1956 their example has been exceeded in various respects by such former paragons of communist orthodoxy as Rumania, Hun-

---

*In 1971 the Polish press was blaming the West German-based Radio Free Europe for inciting the riots of December 1970 in Poland. Unless the RFE license was revoked, the Poles would not ratify the 1970 Treaty, Party organs claimed. Since the license was renewed by the Brandt government until July 1972, the threat may be tested.

gary, and Czechoslovakia. But Poland opened the way to domestic as well as foreign policy changes without incurring the kind of overt Soviet hostility which befell the Yugoslavs in 1948 or the Hungarians in 1956. She was neither ostracized, expelled, nor invaded in consequence of her position.[4]

The changes began when Gomułka and Cyrankiewicz journeyed to Moscow in November 1956 to reestablish Polish-Soviet relations— strained to the breaking point by the events of the Polish October— on a new and more equitable plane. Gomułka demanded and obtained curbs upon Soviet deployment of troops on Polish territory and compensation for past Soviet exploitation of Polish resources—notably coal sold by the Bierut regime at "give-away" prices to the USSR.

In December 1956 a treaty regulating the status of the Soviet armed forces stationed in Poland was signed. The Soviet Union agreed to cancel Polish debts for credit granted to Poland in the 1949–56 period in a sum exceeding one-half billion dollars. The cancellation was actually but a partial restitution to the Poles for many years of international economic exploitation. The Soviets also committed themselves to support "the inviolability of the Polish German frontier on the Oder-Neisse line." Gomułka was allowed an unprecedented appearance before Russia's Supreme Soviet to justify Poland's case for an indigenous and autonomous "path to socialism."

In the early years of Gomułka's regime, Poland still experienced considerable difficulties establishing the legitimacy of her new role among the Communist states. Her policy toward Yugoslavia exemplified both the Polish autonomy and its problems. Over a whole decade Gomułka managed to maintain better relations with Tito than either the Soviet Union or any other Communist state. In January 1957, following a visit by the Yugoslav Vice President to Warsaw, Poland let it be known that she was in full agreement with Yugoslavia on such essentials of "polycentrism" as (1) the legitimacy and desirability of various, individually adapted, paths to the construction of a communist society; (2) nonintervention by one state in the affairs of another and (3) bilateral resolutions of differences. Poland's good relations with maverick Yugoslavia provoked criticism from several other Communist states—Czechoslovakia, Bulgaria, China, and the Soviet Union itself.

The Chinese, who had supported Gomułka's demands for domestic autonomy, were disturbed by his closeness to the "renegade neutralist" Tito as well as by the Polish acceptance of American economic aid and credits. Would Gomułka turn out to be another Nagy, embrace neutralism and abandon Communism? A scheduled visit by Mao Tse

Tung to Warsaw in the summer of 1957 was quietly dropped. By early 1958 Poland had remained virtually the only Communist nation on good terms with Tito. When Khrushchev failed to budge the Yugoslavs from their non-aligned position between East and West, he tried, like Stalin, to ostracize them from the community of Communist nations. In this venture he had least success with the Poles. During the April 1958 Congress of the Communist League of Yugoslavia, the Polish Ambassador, Grocholski, was the only bloc representative who did *not* boycott the meeting. In May the Party's Warsaw daily, *Trybuna Ludu* became the only party organ within the bloc which refused to join in the general attack on the Yugoslavs. This attitude of the Poles led Khrushchev to single them out by his silence at the meeting of the East German Party Congress in July 1958. He attacked the Yugoslavs and did not refer to the Poles, although he had praised the achievements of all the other Communist states.

Another show of Polish independence was occasioned by the tragic execution of Imre Nagy in Hungary. In this case, the Soviets appear to have applied all sorts of pressure—diplomatic, economic, and reportedly even military—to secure expressions of support for the execution of Nagy from the erstwhile satellites. Gomułka found it difficult to appease the Russians inasmuch as the Polish Party press had generally taken a sympathetic view of the Hungarian Revolution and Polish public opinion was unmistakably inflamed by the ultimate harshness of Nagy's punishment. Unlike other bloc leaders, he remained silent for eleven days after the execution on June 17, 1958.

On June 28 Gomułka finally issued an ambiguous statement which criticized Nagy's political past but left out approval of his actual sentence and execution.

Polish attitudes toward China in the 1950s were more sympathetic than the Soviet. At the outset, Gomułka needed and appreciated Chinese supported for the Polish Party's policies of independence or at least autonomy vis à vis the USSR. In 1956 the Chinese were anxious to enhance their own position relative to the Soviet by preaching obliquely against "great power chauvinism." The Poles, in turn, were sympathetic to China's right to develop along its own "road to socialism," and, unlike the Russians, pointedly refrained from criticizing the Chinese in 1958 when the latter embarked on their radical "Great Leap Forward."

Yet, Gomułka had steadfastly affirmed Poland's adherence to the Soviet's peaceful coexistence policy. He denounced Chinese attacks on the Soviet leadership as "slanderous" and "absurd." Like Khrushchev, Gomułka saw communism eventually triumphant by the force of its example, without a recourse to arms. An East-West War would be suicidal for both sides and for mankind, Gomułka maintained. He accused the Chinese of operating on a "double standard": they attacked all attempts at Soviet-U.S. cooperation, yet they themselves had been striving for such cooperation with France.

Gomułka denied that armed revolutionary struggle against "imperialism" was, or could be, the chief slogan of the communist movement in the thermonuclear age, though he conceded that it might still be necessary in "some countries," and to these the Soviet Union and other communist states should render all the help in their power.

He attributed the causes of Chinese behavior to nationalism and frustration at the hands of the United States which—Soviet efforts notwithstanding—made it impossible for the Chinese to enjoy the international influence and status to which they felt themselves justly entitled. But he maintained that the Soviet Union was also justified in not giving the Chinese nuclear weapons because this would encourage proliferation among the "imperialists and nonsocialist states" as well.

To be sure, Gomułka called for efforts to recover the "unity and solidarity of brotherly parties," even if this should turn out to be a lengthy and difficult process. In common with the Rumanians, he was not anxious to narrow down the possibilities of anyone's "deviationism" by overly sweeping condemnations of the Chinese. He had nothing to say in criticism of domestic Chinese policies. Only in the latter part of 1966 and early 1967, in response to the upheaval of China's "cultural revolution" and her internal power struggles, did the Polish Party press finally begin to step up its anti-Mao line, bringing it closer to the more critical Soviet views.

Beyond ideological affinity, the special relationship between the Soviet Union and Poland has been based upon the perception of a common danger from a revival of German power in the west, and upon Soviet willingness and ability to protect Poland from its consequences.

Until the late 1960's, the Polish Communists, with considerable plausibility, had singled out the West German Federal Republic as their international "Enemy Number One." This policy has always had considerable domestic rationale, for the regime found its one solid line of appeal to the Polish people in the maintenance of the Oder-Neisse line as the country's permanent frontier. Poland obviously had a great deal to lose by German demands for a return to pre-World War II frontiers, and the memory of Nazi occupation and Nazi crimes in Poland during the War still remains strong. With these facts in view, the Party for some twenty years attacked West German revanchism, apparent, incipient, and even imaginary. A weak Poland could not resist Germany, and—judging by the experience of 1939 and of Munich—Soviet support was indispensable to stem German ambitions, the Party argued.

At the Fifth Party Congress in 1964, for example, Gomułka attacked virtually all West German leaders, accusing them of plotting agression against Poland and East Germany under the cloak of NATO. He supported East German proposals for a confederation of the two Germanies as a basis for German reunification and indicated that, in the Polish view, reunification was bound to be a long, historical process, feasible only under a general scheme of disarmament and relaxation of tensions in Europe. The best solutions available immediately, Gomułka said, were the conclusion of peace treaties recognizing the *status quo* existence of the two Germanies and of Poland in their present frontiers, and the renunciation of nuclear arms by both German states. He also called for a "normalization of the status of West Berlin" and renewed pledges of Polish-Soviet cooperation. Much of Gomułka's foreign policy presentation was directed against the rearmament of West Germany and toward a "freeze" of nuclear armaments in east central Europe under international inspection.

Polish Party and Government propaganda created and reinforced a sinister and powerful stereotype of West German militarism and imperialism which was a compendium of Polish historical experience, and the real enough horrors of Nazi rule in World War II, reinforced by conceptions drawn from Marxian doctrine. West Germany was pictured as a barely disguised version of Hitler's Third Reich, with powerful financiers, capitalists, and militarists in actual control of policy and bent on the pursuit of the same Nazi objectives at the first propitious opportunity. The much smaller East German Democratic Republic with its Communist regime and under Soviet tutelage was seen as harmless to Poland and useful as a buffer. It would keep West Germany smaller and weaker by its separate existence.

Conciliatory gestures made in the past by West German Chancellors Adenauer, Erhard, and Kiesinger were dismissed as mere "propaganda." To be sure, no West German government had renounced the frontiers of Germany prior to Hitler's acquisitions, until in March 1967 Willy Brandt's Social Democrats had opted for the renunciation of Silesia, Pomerania, and East Prussia, contingent on a peace treaty. Until 1968, however, the frequently repeated assurances by West German leaders that in the future Germany would pursue territorial claims by peaceful means only, and that the solution of territorial questions should be left to a peace conference in which a free and reunited Germany would have a voice, were officially discounted in Warsaw.

West Germany's role in NATO and her demands for nuclear armaments, or a share in the NATO decision-making process involving the
use of nuclear weapons, were widely emphasized in the Polish press.
The gist of the official stereotype presented West Germany as a state
slyly waiting for the right opportunity to set fire to European and world
peace in pursuit of a traditional "Drang Nach Osten." The substantial
currents of West German public opinion expressing a desire for genuine reconciliation with Poland were officially ignored or discounted.
On the other hand, efforts by the Polish Church to achieve better
relations with the West Germans were dubbed treasonable by the
Government and Party spokesmen as recently as Poland's 1966 millennium. The regime charged betrayal of the Polish martyrs of Hitlerite
persecution in Poland! It linked its territorial concerns to a policy of
keeping Germany weak, divided, and disarmed. Reunification was, in
fact, seen as a serious threat to Polish security.[5]

Under Gomułka's leadership, Poland's effort to extend international recognition of the newly acquired possessions on the Oder-
Neisse line among the Western powers was vigorous but, ironically,
until 1970, not very successful. In 1965 Premier Cyrankiewicz journeyed to Paris to meet President de Gaulle but failed to get France's
public support, although, to the consternation of several foreign capi-
tals, Cyrankiewicz publicly thanked de Gaulle for the support which he
alleged the general had given him privately. Chancellor Erhard
promptly announced that this was not the case, and de Gaulle himself
remained silent. In similar efforts, Poland failed to get the backing of
Britain or Italy for her frontiers in various talks held during 1964–66.
The failure was attributable not only to the wide disparity between
Polish and western evaluations of postwar Germany but to the involvement of great power interests and lingering Cold War issues of European and world security. Poland's—and the Soviet Union's—interest
in keeping Germany weak and divided was widely suspect in the West,
even if the powerful emotions accummulated behind it were not un-
reciprocated there.

In September 1967 President de Gaulle made a state visit to Poland.
He received the most enthusiastic and tumultuous reception accorded
any foreign visitor since the War. He repeatedly declared the Oder-
Neisse territories to be "the most Polish of all Polish lands", but he
also suggested that Poland agree to German reunification and loosen
her ties with the Soviet Union. To Gomułka this seemed an unacceptable exchange of a bird in hand for one in the bush. In a speech to the
Sejm he reminded de Gaulle that western alliances did not prove
effective for Poland in 1939 and indicated that Poland was not about

to give up the reality of Soviet and East German backing for the hope of good will on the part of a reunified Germany of the future.

In contrast to the non-committal and equivocal western attitudes, Russia has never wavered in support of Poland's position. In 1958 Marshall Voroshilov travelled throughout Poland, carrying the message of Soviet support against any future German aggression against her. In 1959 Khrushchev himself journeyed extensively through Poland's western territories similarly pledging Soviet assistance to the Poles against West German "militarists and revenge seekers."

On February 14, 1958, Poland's Foreign Minister, Adam Rapacki, proposed his plan for an atom-free central Europe. According to the plan, Poland, Czechoslovakia, West Germany, and East Germany would join to prohibit the manufacture, stockpiling, installation, and operation of nuclear weapons in their territories. On November 4, Rapacki coupled this suggestion with the proposal that its implementation be followed by a reduction of conventional armaments by the participants. On March 28, 1962, he presented the "third version" of this plan to the eighteen member U.N. Disarmament Conference in Geneva, calling for a system of international inspection and control.

The Rapacki proposals in their several versions were not only wholly in accord with Soviet policy for Europe but their presentation by Poland involved a significant upgrading of the Polish position within the Communist Bloc.

Even though Khrushchev had opposed Gomułka's selection as the Polish Party's leader in 1956 and had at first regarded him with an unmistakable suspicion, their relationship grew into one of friendship. Gomułka gradually assumed the role of an elder statesman, advisor, and counselor to Poland's former Russian overlords. In the 1960s Russo-Polish summit meetings grew more frequent. Thus in 1963 Khrushchev and Gomułka exchanged visits in January and November. In January 1964 another Polish-Soviet summit meeting took place in the Polish forest of Białowieża, followed by a Gomułka-Cyrankiewicz visit to Moscow in April, where the Polish leaders were feted at the Kremlin and accorded red-carpet treatment. In a joint communiqué following this conference and a subsequent speech by Khrushchev, the Russians attacked those "who would wish to change existing frontiers," obvious reassurances to Poland of Russian support for the Oder-Neisse frontier in the West. In July Khrushchev attended Warsaw celebrations of the Polish regime's twentieth anniversary.

On October 11, 1964, after Khrushchev was ousted from leadership by Brezhnev and Kosygin, Gomułka publicly praised him instead of joining in the hitherto traditional communist condemnations of fallen leaders. Within a few days of the changes in Moscow, the new Soviet chieftains hurriedly journeyed to Poland, apparently to reassure Gomułka of the continuity of Soviet policy and to explain the removal of Khrushchev. On October 26, the Polish leader finally declared that Khrushchev's ouster was "justified," and he went on to still another conference with Brezhnev and Kosygin in Moscow coincident with the November celebration of the anniversary of the Bolshevik Revolution.

When Gierek replaced Gomułka in December 1970, the Soviet leaders expressed perfunctory public support for him. But the new First Secretary has yet to establish himself in the eyes of the leaders of the Kremlin. The prestige and confidence accorded Gomułka could not be easily gained.

Polish pursuit of Soviet friendship, for international as well as domestic reasons, has not been without its handicaps. The policy has brought about cutbacks in Poland's economic and cultural relations with the United States at one end of the international spectrum, and with Red China at the other. Gomułka's alignment with the Soviet Union and frequent denunciations of American imperialism and NATO may well have been part of the price of survival for his regime in Poland, but they have not been popular with the Polish people. In 1960 and 1964, Gomułka allowed the then Vice-President Nixon and Attorney General Robert F. Kennedy, respectively, to visit Poland. Notwithstanding years of anti-U.S. propaganda, the receptions given to these American leaders by the Polish people in their hundreds of thousands were overwhelmingly enthusiastic and contrasted starkly with the perfunctory welcomes accorded to Soviet and Communist dignitaries. Pro-Russian, anti-Western policies not only ran counter to the sentiments of the Polish people, but as in the case of Czechoslovakia and other East European nations, cut traditional trade links. In the 1940s the absorption of Poland into the Soviet sphere of influence brought about a reorientation of Polish economic life away from the West. Most of Poland's prewar trade was with Western Europe. In 1937 trade with Russia was only about 1 percent of Poland's total foreign trade volume. By 1948 it rose to 22 percent and by 1952 to 32 percent. As of 1969 Polish-Soviet trade accounted for more than one-third of all Polish foreign trade transactions. Where in 1937 the countries of eastern Europe—today's People's Democracies—accounted for only 6 percent of Polish trade, they have contributed about 35 percent since 1952; "other nations" have declined from the preponderant figure of 93 percent in 1937 to about one-third in 1952 and thereafter. The decade of Gomułka's rule did not reverse the "eastern" tendency.

The accomplishments of his regime in foreign trade consist rather in the great expansion of its volume, a substantial increase in the sale of industrial goods abroad, and the significant diversification of that one-third share of Poland's trade which she conducts with the non-communist nations.

Since 1955 Polish imports have risen from 3.7 billion zlotys to 9.9 billion in 1966; exports from 3.6 to 9.1. In 1955 only 13.1 percent of Polish exports represented industrial goods; in 1966 the figure was 35.3 percent. The proportion of Poland's annual industrial output going into exports has virtually doubled.

In increasing her total trade, Poland has opened up some new windows on the world since the 1950s. In Europe she has established substantial economic relations with Yugoslavia, and even with Spain, Portugal, and Greece, all of which, for ideological-political reasons, were shunned by the Polish Stalinist leadership. Notwithstanding all the political differences, even Polish trade with Albania has approximately quadrupled since 1955.

When Gomułka returned to power, West Germany ranked seventh as a source of Polish imports and sixth as a market for Polish exports. Since then, she has become Poland's fifth most important market and sixth principal source of Polish imports. In the 1950s Poland had virtually no trade relations with the nations of Asia, except for China and Pakistan, nor of Africa, except for Nasser's U.A.R. Under Gomułka's rule, Poland expanded trade to ten African and eighteen Asian nations and added five nations in Latin America as well as Australia and New Zealand to her list of trading partners.

In 1959 Poland imported 224.2 million zlotys worth of goods from China. In 1958 she exported goods there valued at 288.6 million. Historically these have been the highest figures attained in Sino-Polish trade. For Poland, this volume of trade made China her third best customer in 1958, behind the USSR and Czechoslovakia, and in 1959 sixth largest source of goods abroad. Since 1961, however, Chinese imports have declined to about 95 million annually and exports to China have averaged even less.

In 1964 the United States was Poland's fourth highest source of imports at 452.8 million, behind Russia, East Germany and Czechoslovakia. In 1965–66, however, American imports averaged less than 150 million zlotys annually, placing the United States, like China, far down the list.

Paradoxically, Poland's most recent foreign difficulties involved neighboring Communist nations. Her international position was being challenged from within, and her system of alliances was threatened by disruption.

Polish relations with most other Communist states probably reached their optimum effectiveness in 1958–59, a period when China, Albania, Yugoslavia, and the Soviet Union could all still be regarded as "friendly," a period when Poland no longer seemed a maverick to the more orthodox communist regimes but not yet reactionary to other still more "liberal" regimes. The first exceptions to this trend were China and Albania when it became increasingly clear that Poland really was a firm follower of Khrushchev's so-called revisionism against Chinese militancy.

The conflict with Albania was intensified by the escape there of the Polish Stalinist Kazimierz Mijał in 1966 and his subsequent regular broadcasts on radio Tirana, beamed at Poland, and full of scathing attacks on the "Gomułka revisionist clique." Albania also became a base for Mijał's new, so-called Communist Party of Poland (KPP), a small and ineffectual but embarrassing challenger for power to the PZPR.[6]

In 1967 and increasingly in 1968, Poland came into open conflict with communism's "liberal" powers, as well as with the "arch-conservatives."

In January 1967, Rumania proceeded to establish diplomatic relations with the West German Federal Republic while also maintaining her relations with Communist East Germany. Ostensibly, it seemed that West Germany was making a concession to the Rumanians, inasmuch as the so-called Hallstein doctrine of 1955 had heretofore committed West Germany to non-recognition of those states (other than the USSR) which maintained diplomatic relations with East Germany.* Poland, however, regarded this development as a threat to her own position inasmuch as the Rumanians did not exact those political "preconditions" from the West Germans which Poland considers essential. On March 1, 1967, Gomułka himself formulated the Polish position thus:[7]

"We have never refused to normalize relations with the German Federal Republic and we continue to be ready for such normalization as long as Bonn recognizes the actual facts that constitute European reality—that is, the existence of two sovereign German states, the inviolability of the existing state frontiers of Europe—and provided it issues a declaration that the Munich diktat has been invalid since it was signed, and renounces the possession or copossession of nuclear weapons."

---

*To the West Germans the GDR had been merely the Soviet-occupied zone of Germany, not another German state.

In light of the Rumanian action, the Poles feared that their insistence on the recognition of the Oder-Neisse frontier might no longer be supported by other East European regimes eager to join the diplomatic "bandwagon," and that West Germany would gradually succeed in diplomatically isolating Poland without making any concessions at all. The regime responded to this threat by drawing even closer to East Germany and the Soviet Union as the two powers which have been most steadfast in support of the Polish claims; it also attempted to reinforce its alliances and counter West German diplomacy, with Czechoslovakia, Hungary and Bulgaria. In March 1967, special, bilateral treaties of mutual assistance, directed against the West Germans, were signed between Poland and East Germany as well as between Poland and Czechoslovakia. In April a Treaty with Bulgaria ensued. Following inter-bloc consultations, it appeared in the spring of 1967 that West German efforts for a *detente* and a reestablishment of diplomatic relations with Hungary and Bulgaria would be temporarily, at least, blocked. But if Rumania's actions proved too disquieting for Poland, the internal "liberalization" in Czechoslovakia—highlighted by the ouster of President Antonin Novotny in January 1968—soon cast the Polish-Czechoslovak Pact of March 1967 into doubt. Less than a year after its conclusion, the Czech press and various personages in the new Prague regime were calling for reexamination and "normalization" of relations with West Germany. It appeared to the Poles that Czechoslovakia might soon follow the Rumanian example after all and that economic and political reforms within that country would be combined with futher erosion, if not abandonment, of the Warsaw Pact and of bilateral arrangements guaranteeing the Polish frontiers.

Compounding the international crisis, the Polish Party's campaign against "Zionism," begun after the Arab-Israeli War in June 1967, became an object of increasing denunciations by the Czechoslovak and Yugoslav party organs. It was being described and condemned as unseemly and un-Marxian anti-Semitism by two important, hitherto friendly, "fraternal parties."

All these developments spurred the Polish Communist regime to support Soviet pressures for a halt in Czechoslovakia's internal liberalization. Gomułka's Poland joined with East Germany and the USSR in calling together a conference in Dresden on March 23, 1968, against the background of ominous reports of Soviet troop movements in the vicinity of the Czech frontiers. The conference was attended by party leaders from Hungary and Bulgaria as well as the "northern tier powers": Russia, Poland, and East Germany. The new Czech Communist Party Secretary, Alexander Dubcek, was asked to explain the policies of his regime to other Warsaw Pact Party leaders. Among the latter, only Rumania was not represented. She had denounced all attempts at foreign interference in the domestic affairs of communist nations. The conference ended with a communique affirming the participants' faith in the "continued progress of socialist construction" under the new regime in Czechslovakia but this faith proved short-lived. Another conference was convened in Warsaw in mid-July, this time warning the Czechs about alleged "imperialist machinations and subversion" in their midst. The crisis was underscored by widespread reports that Soviet troops which had entered Czechoslovakia as participants in Warsaw Pact maneuvers in June were exceedingly slow in making their departure.

On August 20, 1968, Polish troops assisted those of Russia and several Warsaw Pact powers in the invasion of Czechoslovakia. The liberal-reformist regime of Aleksander Dubcek was quickly destroyed by overwhelming force of arms. A great turn-about in Polish policy had taken place. The Communist regime of Poland which had been the harbinger of reform in Eastern Europe under the leadership of Władysław Gomułka in 1956 became one of the principal persecutors of reform in 1968. Polish foreign policy, in its Soviet orbit, had travelled full circle from the joint declaration with Yugoslavia about the rights of polycentrism in 1957 to their denial in 1968.

In the aftermath of Czechoslovakia, virtually nothing was left of the independence and liberalism which Gomułka had symbolized to Poland and the world twelve years earlier. Ironically, the rapproachment with West Germany in 1970 seemed to make the 1968 invasion of Czechoslovakia all the less justifiable in terms of a Polish *raison d'etat*. Did Gomułka really come to fear the effect of Dubcek's example on Poland? Or, pressed by Moczar, was he simply too dependent on the USSR not to go along with it?

In any case, at the end of the decade, Poland's foreign policy was more closely linked to that of the Soviet Union than at any time since the Polish October. Gomułka's pliancy toward the Soviets seemed directly correlated to his growing weakness at home. Whether the new and still precarious leadership of Gierek would reestablish a more independent role for Poland remained to be seen.

NOTES

1. See M. Dewar, *Soviet Trade in Eastern Europe, 1945–1949* (London, 1951); Nicholas Halasz, *In the Shadow of Russia: Eastern Europe in the*

Postwar World (New York, 1959); Victor Winston, "The Polish Bituminous Coal-Mining Industry," *American Slavic and East European Review*, XV, February 1956, pp. 38–70; Stanley J. Żyzniewski, "Coal in Poland's Economy and Foreign Policy," *Journal of Central European Affairs*, XIX, October 1959, pp. 260–274.

2. See Kazimierz Grzybowski, *The Socialist Commonwealth of Nations* (New Haven, 1964); Stanislaw Wellisz, *The Economies of the Soviet Bloc* (New York, 1964); Jan Wszelaki, *Comunist Economic Strategy and the Role of East Central Europe*, Washington, D.C., National Planning Association, 1959; Alexander Bregman "Whither Russia: The U.S.S.R. and Eastern Europe," *Problems of Communism*, May–June 1967, vol. XVI, No. 3, pp. 50–54.

3. See Piotr S. Wandycz, "The Soviet System of Alliances in East Central Europe," *Journal of Central European Affairs* XVI, July 1956, pp. 177–184.

4. Cf. Adam Bromke, "Poland's Role in the Loosening of the Communist Bloc," *International Journal*, vol. XX, Autumn 1965, pp. 484–509.

5. See Władysław Gomułka, "Policy of the Polish People's Republic," *Foreign Affairs*, XXXVIII, April 1960, pp. 402–418; and also Władysław Tykociński, "An Interview," *East Europe*, vol. 15, No. 11, November 1966, pp. 9–16.

6. Cf. "The Chinese Road to Socialism for Russia and Poland," *Survey*, No. 63, April 1967, pp. 139–158.

7. Radio Warsaw Speech.

7

Conclusion

THE YEARS OF Gomułka's leadership of the PZPR (1956–1970) represented a period of transition for Poland. The "Muscovite" leadership of Bierut and Berman had steered the country in the direction of an Orwellian monolith patterned on the Soviet example; Gomułka first reversed this tendency, and then, in effect, froze the political system somewhere between the most repressive communist models of the past and the more flexible, liberal, and prosperous ones of the current era.[1]

Admittedly, the Party in Poland never achieved a position of *total power* over its social and political environment. Even in the heyday of Stalinism it shared the control of the economy with an "obstreperous" Polish peasant and the dissemination of information and socio-political ideals with a vigorous and powerful Church.[2]

Faced with an acute shortage of skilled and politically reliable operatives, the Party resorted in the 1940s and 1950s to the services of officers, judges, administrators, teachers, and sundry experts of prewar vintage whose Communist loyalties were highly suspect. Thus, many nominal Party controls—over the armed forces, for example— were in practice far less total and dependable than they appeared on paper.

Since the return of Gomułka, pluralism within the Party itself, the partial and equivocal nature of the leaders' powers, had become more evident. In 1967–68 Polish readers could choose up sides in the Party press between those sympathetic to to the Party's First Secretary, in *Polityka,* and those supporting the Police Chief in *Żołnierz Wolności.* Television viewers could see General Moczar attack Gomułka for his "softness toward Zionism." In the period of the "Polish October" and in 1957 the dissensions within the Party were, if anything, even more visible. In addition, much of the *de facto* pluralism of the Polish political system has always been more apparent to "insiders" than to the general public in Poland and abroad.[3]

A certain amount of conflict, interplay of interests, and mutual adjustment has taken place among the administrative and technical organs serving the regime: the ministries, departments, and bureaus jockeying for funds, for jurisdictional controls, personnel, or the allocation of favorable economic targets for themselves. These conflicts have played their part in diversifying a would-be monolith. For while government organizations all claim 100 percent loyalty to the regime and eschew any outwardly political claims of their own, the rivalry among them forces the Party leadership to bargain and compromise in various aspects of policy, particularly in its execution. The claims of the administrators and the technicians are generally formulated behind the scenes and without publicity, but they are important in the final determination of the regime's policies nonetheless.[4]

Because of the increasingly rigid orthodoxy and controls which Gomułka embraced, he had lost virtually all of his popularity of the 1956–57 period. Gomułka's domestic reforms had been something of a half-way house, even initially. He ended the terrorism of the security police, but he did not abolish censorship. He increased wages and the flow of consumer goods over the pre-1956 levels, but he retained an exasperating imbalance between investment in heavy industry on the one hand and consumer products on the other. He allowed some decentralization in Polish planning but not as much as the Hungarians, Czechs, Yugoslavs, and Rumanians have undertaken: he allowed worker participation in industrial management in 1956 only to dilute and nullify its effects in 1959. The ideological and political struggle against the Church was not abandoned. Collectivization "by force" and "for now" was shelved, but continued emphasis on the superirority of socialized forms of agricultural production has maintianed uneasiness among the peasantry.

The Party's encouragement of the so-called Agricultural Circles in which peasants, with substantial government aid, pool resources for collective cultivation of individual plots won few converts: about 0.5 percent of arable land is now linked by such arrangements. But it was enough to maintain an undercurrent of tension in the countryside and spur peasant bitterness at the regime's discriminatory investment policies.

Another such measure was a November 1967 decision of the Party's Central Committee which called for "pensioning-off" farm owners whom the regime judged to be "inefficient" or "incompetent" opera-

tors. The lands thus acquired would be added to the state domain, and
the Party resolution estimated that the measure would bring 30 percent of arable land into state ownership by 1975.

Clearly, not all of Poland's economic troubles have been of the
Government's making. Polish foreign trade has not expanded as fast
as it might have because of Common Market competition in the West.
The prices of Poland's chief export, coal, have declined over the years.
Costs of machinery and equipment purchased abroad and needed for
her own industrial expansion have risen. Exports have not kept pace
with imports. Wages, although low, have risen faster than productivity.
There have also been some naturally poor harvests in the 1960's. But
rigid and unrealistic planning and government inefficiency in the execution of plans have played a major role in the over-all failure of
the Polish economy to assure a better standard of living to the nation.

In an effort to improve the state of the economy, Gomułka promised
in August 1965 a policy of reforms, with emphasis on what one of
Poland's leading planners called a "qualitative advance." The new
approach was to stress the quality and assortment of goods and services produced, not merely or mainly the volume. The value of the
output was to be judged in terms of the relative costs of production,
the impact on Poland's foreign trade position, and the extent to which
it relied on domestically available raw materials. Greater use was to be
made of scientific research, computers, and mathematical models to
improve the planning process; and an increased role was to be given
the Conferences of Worker Self-Government in all phases of economic
planning.

That all these promises and hopes proved unfounded became clear
in December 1970, when Polish workers and consumers forced the
ouster of Gomułka. Strikes, demonstrations, and ultimately large-scale
violence testified to the failures of the Polish economy under communism.

Having aroused high hopes for change in 1956, Gomułka brought
Poland to the abyss of 1970, where even the notoriously repressive
East German Communists, not to mention Hungarians and Rumanians, could boast a more pragmatic, flexible, efficient, and ultimately
humane administration of the national economy.* And the departure
of Gomułka left the PZPR a weak, divided, and tragically demoralized

---

*A few weeks after Gomułka's downfall on the heels of his sudden 20 percent price
increase decree, East Germany announced a 20 percent reduction of most consumer
prices.

organization, continuing the trends of the late 1960s.

In early 1972 Edward Gierek's hold on power within the Party and the policies he would pursue were still in doubt. It seemed likely that Gierek would seek to ease the plight of the Polish consumers, decentralize the economy, and perhaps raise its productivity through more effective management and incentives. His talks with Polish workers and announcements about reviving the role of the Sejm all indicated a wish to inject more dialogue and more responsiveness to popular opinion into the process of government. But there were many obstacles: the "hard line" enclave, the uncertain tolerance of the Russians, the legacy of years of economic mismanagement, and the inertia of Polish bureaucracy. The mood of the workers was one of anger, resentment, and suspicion. They remembered many previous promises and were understandably disillusioned. Yet, if Gierek failed to end labor unrest, no economic program, however sound, could succeed. The Party's grasp on power, Brezhnev Doctrine apart, was a tenuous one.

December 1970, like October 1956, demonstrated that even though lacking free and open elections, the people of Poland could bring about significant changes of their rulers and of the policies they pursue. To be sure, this method of change required the willingness of many thousands of people to risk death and injury before tanks and guns. And it required the sacrifice of many lives. It was also a crude form of changing leaders and policies—twice in fourteen years. The Party was able, on each occasion, to make concessions of a discretionary sort.

Admittedly, if Gomułka had not been replaced by Gierek in 1970, and if Gierek had not raised the minimum wage, or increased social security benefits, or froze prices, strikes and riots might have swelled into a popular revolution against the Party. In such an event Soviet intervention would have been both likely, and from the standpoint of keeping the Party in power, necessary. But, once the worst eventualities were averted by a new leadership, with concessions, and some symbolic gestures, the Party could well turn its back on all sorts of popular aspirations. Its monopoly of arms, its control of legal and administrative sanctions and of the communications media made it easy for the PZPR to reserve its "responsiveness" only for those occasions on which despair drove the masses to insurrection, with all the attendant risks and penalties that oppositionists face in dictatorial political systems. After all, the December 13 price decree which overnight, without public warning or debate, raised Polish living costs by nearly 20 percent, was an eloquent testimonial to the capricious power of the Party's dictatorship.[5] It represented the quintessence of all those evils which the Polish students had condemned and fought against in 1968.

The shock of the December decree and of the violent popular reaction to it prompted the new Gierek-Jaroszewicz leadership to give an unusual emphasis to the need for dialogue between the Party and the workers, the officials and the people. Gomułka's aloofness and authoritarianism were officially assailed.

For Polish Communism to survive on its own, without reliance on the threat of Soviet intervention, the Party will probably have to explore new directions. This seems to be the implication of its quarter century experiment during which the PZPR has managed to capture genuine popular following briefly and only once—when it seemed least orthodox, least doctrinaire, least Russophile.

Without recourse to free elections or scientifically sampled polls common in the western world, it is obviously difficult to establish precisely the attitudes of Polish public opinion. Direct evidence of a fairly impressionistic character may be gleaned from public demonstrations, the reports of official press, and the conversations and accounts of foreign visitors and of Poles visiting abroad.

Some idea of the attitudinal impact of Communist rule may be gleaned from audience research surveys carried out by Radio Free Europe several years ago.[6] Since the survey samples involved were relatively small and drawn from persons who either visited the West or actually fled Poland, their results are of somewhat limited value and must be viewed with caution. Nevertheless, they provide interesting clues on an important subject and seem to confirm some of the more recent and less tangible expressions of Polish public opinion. The surveys tested attitudes among several hundred persons on a set of issues in 1958–60 and again on the same issues in 1961–62.

The findings of Radio Free Europe surveys indicated very minimal over-all support for Communism in Poland. There appeared to be a substantial measure of recognition for some of the reforms and some of the social and economic achievements carried out under Party auspices. But this recognition did not, as yet, translate into majority support of the regime in *any* significant section of Polish society. While many in the R.F.E. samples approved various, specific Communist actions, an overwhelming majority rejected "communism" itself as "a bad idea badly carried out." In 1958, 75 percent of those polled expressed this wholly negative view; in 1960, 61 percent did.

Insofar as the specific policies were concerned, the regime paradoxically both failed and succeeded most on bread-and-butter issues. It seems to have won a measure of recognition for actions which, like land reform and the extension of public education, have promoted welfare and equality. It has also flattered Polish national pride with its accomplishments in industrialization. But it has failed most damagingly in improving individual living standards nearly enough or in proportion to popular expectations. Even above such values as political and personal freedom, this is what the largest number of R.F.E. respondents found most praiseworthy about the West.

In contrast 79 percent of the respondents in 1958–60 regarded the economic failures of the Polish regime as its most serious faults. These included shortages of consumer goods, low wages and high prices, the housing shortage, and the inevitable queues. 57 percent singled out economic failures in the 1961–62 survey.

One of the most significant areas of complaint against the regime —second in importance to economic deprivation of the consumer— has been the impact of bureaucracy. Inefficient, corrupt, and all-pervasive bureaucratic controls were the target of chief complaint by one out of four respondents in the 1961–62 survey.

The most popular aspects of Communist policies since 1945, judging by both surveys and all types of respondents, were the extension of free education and social welfare measures in that order. Asked what measures taken by the regime should be continued regardless of the political system, 33 percent of the 1958–60 sample favored free education; 25 percent agreed on the welfare state; industrialization was third with 13 percent, agrarian reform was fourth with 11 percent. On the other hand, 19 percent thought nothing at all was worth continuing.

One of the by-products of the Gomułka regime in the 1960s appeared to be a growing popular "disengagement" from politics, a mood which reflected in part a fatalistic acceptance of the continuance of Communist rule for an indefinite period; in part an implicit rejection of the system; and in part also a somewhat lessened fear and resentment toward the regime in response to the policy of relaxation which it had followed during that period. According to R.F.E. surveys, most Poles would have preferred a parliamentary democracy on a western model to any other political system. Very few of them opted for the return of the authoritarian regime of the pre-1939 period. Few, however, expected any major changes within the foreseeable future which would make the overthrow of Communism possible. And among those who thought that life in Poland under Red rule "would continue to improve," there were many who saw this trend as occurring *despite*, not *because* of Communist policies.

Ideological alienation and an essentially static view of Poland's international position on the doorstep of the Soviet Union seemed to produce a kind of "internal psychological emigration" which paralleled the outlook of many Poles in the partitioned Poland of the nineteenth century. The young, in particular, appeared to find an outlet for their interests and energies not *in* but *apart* from politics.

Many of the trends reported by R.F.E. are substantiated by more recent, and still fragmentary, findings of Polish sociologists. Membership figures in the PZPR and its affiliates also offer a supportive index. As of 1965 only 9 percent of PZPR members were under 25 years of age. Among university students only about 2 percent were Party members. Fewer than 15 percent belonged to the Party's two youth leagues: the urban ZMS and the rural ZMW.

In a poll taken at the university of Warsaw in 1961 by Polish sociologists, 72 percent of the students professed sympathy for "some form of socialism"; but only 18.4 percent described themselves as "Marxists" while 65 percent described themselves as adhering to the Catholic faith! 89 percent of those "favorable to socialism" said they actually favored "unrestricted private enterprise in trade!" Clearly, what these youths understood by "socialism" could hardly have been any comfort to the Party.

Moreover, political interest of any kind among students was found to be declining. Where in 1958, 29 percent said they were not interested at all whether the world was moving toward "socialism" or away from it, in 1961, 40 percent did not care about it. Where in 1958, 45 percent reported politics as a very rare subject of discussion with friends, 56 percent did so in 1961. Yet, in 1961, 84 percent of the students said they were content with their way of life, while only 75 percent said so in 1958. The number of those willing to risk their lives for religion between 1958 and 1961 dropped from a half to a third. It thus seemed that a rise in political involvement among youth was generally apt to coincide with increased discontent.[7] The 1968 protest movement among university students in Warsaw, Poznan, Krakow, Lodz, and other centers of learning corroborated this finding.

Could a change of policies by the Party, in a renewal of the spirit of October 1956 or pursuit of the promises of 1970, bring it a larger measure of acceptance? Is the Party really capable of such a change?

With all its limitations, the method of change by mass action was a recognized fact of political life in Poland in 1972. It had to be reckoned with in future policy making by the Party. It also gave Poland a status unique among the Communist bloc states. Only in Hungary in 1956 did mass action bring about a dramatic leadership change, and this was largely nullified by Soviet intervention. In Czechoslovakia, Rumania, East Germany and Bulgaria as well as the USSR itself, no such changes ever resulted from popular demonstrations. There was no doubt that Poland continued to present a formidable challenge to her Communist rulers and their foreign mentors.

The fading Mieczysław Moczar represents one alternative to the Party's present isolation from the bulk of the Polish people. He would probably reconstitute the highly authoritarian Communist political system, not by relaxing Party controls but by giving them more of an indigenous, Polish-nationalist, "patriotic" foundation and thereby presumably making them more palatable to more Poles. Essentially, this course has been pursued already by the ex-fascist, Bolesław Piasecki, but in an obviously subordinate and limited role. Conceivably, at least, Moczar could balance his unyielding insistence on Party rule and his intolerance of opposition by more pragmatic economic and social policies. He would thus be able to appeal both to the Party bureaucrats and their Soviet backers, as well as to the Polish people as a whole.

But he and the Partisans could hardly expect to win lasting general public support by merely coupling Marxism with the slogans of anti-Semitism and patriotism. Such slogans did not suffice for the prewar Polish National Democrats when Jews and other ethnic minorities presented much more substantial targets than they do nowadays. What Moczar and his supporters, however, would do in other areas of policy, if installed in power, is not so clear.

Another alternative is the resurgence of revisionism, recently so vigorously repressed in the "anti-Zionist" campaign. The success of revisionism within the Party might result either in the preservation of some of the old political forms of Communism with a new *de facto* content or even ultimately, as the Russians have feared, in the total erosion of the revolutionary regime.

The reformist-revisionist potential within the PZPR is obscured by a lack of articulation among the Party's top ranks. The current intra-party conflicts appear to be taking place between "conservatives" and "arch-conservatives," or perhaps among "conservatives," "reactionaries," and those of a mildly "liberal" persuasion. The trends within the Party and in the country as a whole are almost certainly at odds with respect to "revisionism." Yet, the contrast could be readily exaggerated. The Party's rank-and-file is simply too numerous, often too hastily and superficially assembled, too little socialized into genuine beliefs about the Party's programs and ideology to remain immune to various eroding or "alien" influences. The lower echelons of the PZPR are made up of men and women for whom the membership represents a variety of small-scale self-interests, rather than an ideological crusade or even great personal stakes of power, fame, or the advantages of wealth if not of wealth itself. These people necessarily reflect the environment from which they have sprung. In the ingestion of Poland's historic, national, and religious traditions into the communist apparatus the former represents the elephant and the latter the mouse. Admittedly, the impact of the rank-and-file on Party policy is generally much less than that of the full-time bureaucrats, the Party "aparatchiki." But given propitious international and domestic circumstances, the latent revisionism at the bottom and middle rungs of the Party structure could readily make itself felt at the top.

The top leadership of the PZPR is a bureaucracy with an immense vested interest in monopolizing power. Its interests are substantial, clear-cut, and tangible. It is wary of "revisionism" because in practice revisionism would mean, at the very least, a *diminution* of jobs, perquisites, and influence which are now wholly theirs to command. Thus there is a long-term, "secular" bureaucratic disposition against it, and it has been historically reinforced by Soviet backing. Ordinarily, it would favor a Moczar alternative to a revisionist one. But this is not always feasible. The recurrence of large-scale domestic opposition combined with a further decrease in Soviet influence could make some surprising converts to "revisionism" even among the present members of the Polish Politburo.

Power-oriented Communist politicians have also been pragmatists. Ex-Premier Józef Cyrankiewicz, for example, in 1939 was a democratic socialist; in 1945 a Communist collaborator; in 1950 a Stalinist; in 1956 a "liberal" Communist, and in 1968 a clearly "conservative" one. The temptations to "back a winner" must not be underestimated. In the final analysis, Polish revisionism—suspect in the Kremlin as a liquidator of communism and a restorer of capitalism—faces its most crucial test in the attitude of the Soviet Union. The most popular alternatives in Poland may well be least popular in the USSR, and Poland's geography precludes the independence possible for a Yugoslavia, Albania, or even Rumania.

The PZPR has now held power for nearly twenty-eight years since the Polish Committee of National Liberation was installed by the Russians in Lublin. It has yet to establish itself as an indigeneous, legitimate regime in the eyes of the Polish people, notwithstanding all its efforts and all its accomplishments.

In the face of the Polish people's traditionally western political-cultural aspirations, their individualism, love of the land, religiosity, mistrust of Russia, and last but not least the desire for a better and richer life, the Party's prospects of gaining genuine popular acceptance still seem remote.

NOTES

1. See e.g., Frank Gibney, *The Frozen Revolution; Poland: A Study in Communist Decay* (New York, 1959); and Irena Penzik, *Ashes to the Taste* (New York, 1961).
2. On models of communist polities see among others A. G. Meyer, "The Comparative Study of Communist Political Systems," *Slavic Review*, XXVI, no. 1, 1967, pp. 3–12; H. Gordon Skilling, "Interest Groups and Communist Politics," *World Politics*, XVIII, April 1966, pp. 435–51; R. C. Tucker, "On the Comparative Study of Communism," *World Politics*, XIX, January 1967, pp. 242–57., and A. J. Groth, "The Isms in Totalitarianism," *American Political Science Review*, vol. 58, No. 4, December 1964, pp. 888–901.
3. See e.g., Jerzy Mond and Robert Richter, "Writers and Journalists as a Pressure Group in Eastern Europe," *Polish Review*, vol. XI, no. 1, winter 1966, pp. 92–108.
4. Cf. John A. Armstrong, "Sources of Administrative Behavior: Some Soviet and West European Comparisons," *American Political Science Review*, LIX, September 1965, pp. 643–55. See also Bogdan Czaykowski, "Literatura i Polityka w Polsce," *Kultura* (Paris) No. 5/260, May 1969, pp. 89–99 for an account of Party controls of writers and their modest reciprocal leverage against the Party.
5. Cf. A. J. Groth, *Comparative Politics: A Distributive Approach* (New York, 1971), chapter I, pp. 17–24.
6. Radio Free Europe, Audience Research, *Some Aspects of the Attitudinal and Political Climate in Poland* (Attitude Survey II), Munich, Germany, 1963; and Radio Free Europe, Audience Research, *Poland's New Generation*, Munich, Germany, 1963.
7. See Jan Nowak, "Poland's Young Rebels," *Eastern Europe*, vol. 15, No. 4, April 1966, pp. 16–22.

Bibliographical
Essay

To THOSE INTERESTED in further reading about modern Poland, the author offers these necessarily brief recommendations. For a general persepctive of Poland's history prior to the Communist seizure of power, the accounts of Oscar Halecki, *A History of Poland* (New York: Roy Publishers, Inc., 1943); Henryk Frankel's brief *Poland: The Struggle for Power, 1772–1939* (London: L. Drummond, Ltd., 1946); and Hans Roos, *A History of Modern Poland* (London: Eyre and Spottiswoode, 1966) are very helpful. On the domestic politics of the interwar era (1919–1939), Raymond Buell's *Poland: Key to Europe* (New York: Alfred A. Knopf, 1939) and Joseph Rothschild's *Pilsudski's Coup d'etat* (New York: Columbia University Press, 1966) are eminently perceptive and readable. Stephan Horak's *Poland and Her National Minorities, 1919–1939* (New York: Vantage Press, 1961) contains a wealth of data on one of Poland's most serious pre-1939 political problems.

Several books on Poland's foreign policy before World War II supply rich background material to the tragic debacle of 1939. Among these are Roman Dębicki's *Foreign Policy of Poland, 1919–1939* (New York: Praeger, 1962); Josef Korbel, *Poland Between East and West: Soviet and German Diplomacy Toward Poland 1919–1933* (Princeton, N.J.: Princeton University Press, 1963); B. B. Budurowycz, *Polish-Soviet Relations, 1932–1939* (New York: Columbia University Press, 1963); and Piotr S. Wandycz, *Soviet-Polish Relations, 1917–1921* (Cambridge, Mass.: Harvard Univeristy Press, 1969).

On the origins and history of the Communist movement in Poland, the study by M. K. Dziewanowski, *The Communist Party of Poland* (Cambridge, Mass.: Harvard University Press, 1959) is indispensable. For comparative purposes, R. V. Burks' *The Dynamics of Communism in East-*

ern Europe, (Princeton, N. J.: Princeton University Press, 1961) is also very useful.

On the complex process of Poland's diplomatic-military ingestion into the Soviet sphere of influence, the following books may be suggested: Edward J. Rozek, *Allied Wartime Diplomacy: A Pattern in Poland* (New York: John Wiley & Sons, 1958); Stanislaw Mikołajczyk, *The Pattern of Soviet Domination* (London: S. Low, Marston, 1948); Arthur Bliss Lane, *I Saw Poland Betrayed* (Indianapolis: The Bobbs-Merrill Co., 1948); and Stefan Korbonski, *Fighting Warsaw* (New York: Funk and Wagnalls, 1968).

As for the politics of Communist Poland in the years 1945–1971, many of the topics covered in our volume are discussed with greater depth and variety in several important books of the last two decades. These include Oskar Halecki, ed., *Poland* (New York: Praeger, 1957); Czeslaw Milosz, *The Captive Mind* (New York: Vintage Books, 1953); Konrad Syrop, *Spring in October: The Story of the Polish Revolution 1956* (London: Weidenfeld and Nicolson, 1957); Frank Gibney's *The Frozen Revolution* (New York: Farrar, Straus and Cudahy, 1959); Hansjakob Stehle, *The Independent Satellite: Society and Politics in Poland Since 1945* (New York: Praeger, 1965); Richard F. Staar, *Poland, 1944–1962* (Baton Rouge: Louisiana State University Press, 1962); Adam Bromke, *Poland's Politics: Idealism vs. Realism* (Cambridge, Mass.: Harvard University Press, 1967); Richard Hiscocks, *Poland, Bridge for the Abyss?* (London: Oxford University Press, 1963).

Among the most recent books on Poland of a rather general, survey character are Konrad Syrop's *Poland* (London: Hale, 1968); James F. Morrison's *The Polish People's Republic* (Baltimore: Johns Hopkins University Press, 1968); William Woods, *Poland: Eagle in the East* (New York: Hill and Wang, 1968); and Nicholas Bethell, *Gomułka: His Poland, His Communism* (New York: Holt, Rinehart and Winston, 1969).

More specialized useful studies include John M. Montias, *Central Planning in Poland* (New Haven: Yale University Press, 1962); Alfred Zauberman, *Industrial Progress in Poland, Czechoslovakia and East Germany, 1937–1962* (London: Oxford University Press, 1964); and T. P. Alton *et al., Polish National Income and Product* (New York: Columbia University Press, 1965).

For those interested in relating Polish Communism to the Soviet and other East European varieties, both in terms of institutions and policies, the following are particularly appropriate: Zbigniew Brzezinski, *The Soviet Bloc: Unity and Conflict,* rev. and enl, ed. (Cambridge, Mass.: Harvard University Press, 1967); Vladimer Gsovski and Kazimierz Grzybowski, *Government, Law and Courts in the Soviet Union and Eastern*

Europe (New York: Praeger, 1959); Kazimierz Grzybowski, *The Socialist Commonwealth of Nations* (New Haven: Yale University Press, 1964); Gordon Skilling, *The Governments of Communist East Europe* (New York: Thomas Y. Crowell Company, 1966); and W. W. Kulski, *The Soviet Regime: Communism in Practice*, 4th ed. (Syracuse, N. Y.: Syracuse University Press, 1963).

For those who read Polish, the government daily, *Życie Warszawy*, the PZPR daily, *Trybuna Ludu*, and the PZPR monthly organ, *Nowe Drogi*, are particularly valuable: so is the emigré Polish quarterly published in Paris, *Kultura*.English language periodicals featuring information and articles on Poland include *Polish Review; Eastern European Economics; East Europe: A Monthly Review of East European Affairs; East Europe: An International Magazine; Slavic Review; Problems of Communism; Canadian Slavic Studies;* and *Slavonic Review.* From time to time valuable articles on Polish politics have appeared in the *Review Of Politics, Political Science Quarterly, Survey,* and the now defunct *Journal of Central European Affairs.*

Index

Adenauer, Konrad, 127
Africa, 131
Agricultural policy, 101–102, 137–138
AK (Home Army), 14, 16, 60–61
Albania, 131, 132, 144
AL (People's Army), 14
Albrecht, Jerzy, 29
Almond, G., 22, 23
Alton, T. P., 116, 148
Anders, Władysław, 14
Anti-Semitism, 9–10, 71–75, 106
Apanasiewicz, N., 117
Armstrong, J. A., 145
Atlantic Charter, 16
Australia, 131
Austraia, 6, 8

Balicki, Zygmunt, 7
Barwicz, Romuald, 79
BBWR (Non-Partisan Bloc for Coopera-
tion with the Government), 11
Beck, Colonel J., 11, 20
Beck, C., 79
Beria, L., 62
Berling, Zygmunt, 15
Berman, Jakub, 62, 63, 67, 69, 72, 120
Bethell, N,, 148
Bierut, Bolesław, 14, 48, 49, 50, 51, 62,
69, 78, 116, 119
Bliss-Lane, Arthur, 23, 47, 148
Blit, L., 95
Bór-Komorowski, General Tadeusz, 16,
23
Brandt, Willy, 122, 123, 127
Bregman, A., 135

Brezhnev, Leonid, 74, 118, 129, 130
Bromke, Adam, 22, 135, 148
Brzezinski, Z., 70, 148
Budurowycz, B. B., 147
Buell, R. L., 23, 147
Buhler, N., 117
Bulgaria, 118, 120, 121, 124, 133
Buraszkiewicz, J., 30
Burks, R. V., 147
Burski, A., 30
Butler, D. E., 47
Byelorussia, 2, 9, 20

Cantril, H., 23
Casimir, the Great, 3
Caritas, 89–90
China, 124, 125, 126, 130, 131, 132
Chrypiński, V. C., 47
Church, persecution of, 82–83, 84–86
Church-State relations, 80–94
Churchill, W. S., 16, 18, 23
Ciechanowski, Jan, 23
Ciołkosz, Adam, 79
Civic attitudes, 9, 22
Communist Party: KPP, 12–13, 48
   PPR, 14–16, 18–20, 48, 58, 60
   PZPR, 48–79
   organization, 53–56
   Central Committee, 54–55
   Politburo, 27, 54–55
   Secretariat, 55–56
Constitution, 1921, 11, 60
Constitution, 1935, 11, 60
Constitution, 1952, 25–27
Council of Ministers, 27–28, 29–30

Council of Mutual Economic Assistance (COMECON), 120, 123
Council of State, 26–27, 28
Courts, 41–46
Cultural policies, 103–106
Cyrankiewicz, J., 19, 26, 51–52, 54, 55, 63, 72, 86, 124, 128, 129, 144
Czaykowski, B., 145
Czechoslovakia, 61, 73, 74, 89, 98, 106, 118, 120, 121, 122, 123, 124, 129, 131, 133, 134

Debicki, R., 23, 147
December (1970) riots, 40, 51, 75–76
De Gaulle, Charles, 88, 128
Denmark, 75, 106
Dewar, M., 134
Dinka, F., 95
Djilas, Milovan, 68, 113
Dmowski, Roman, 7, 8, 9, 10, 22, 69, 92, 119
Dominican Republic, 35
Drewnowski, J., 117
Dubcek, Alexander, 133, 134
Dyboski, Roman, 22
Dziewanowski, M. K., 22, 58, 78, 147

Economy: before World War II, 11–12, 98–99
   under Communist rule, 98–102, 106–111
Ergang, R., 22
Elections, 11, 13, 19, 31–36
Erhard, Ludwig, 127
Estreicher, Stanisław, 21
Ethnic problems (see also Anti-Semitism), 2, 3, 4, 6, 9–11

Falanga, 90
Farrell, R. B., 79
Feis, Herbert, 21
Fejgin, S., 46, 72
Fejto, F., 117
FON (Front of National Unity) 31, 34, 35
Foreign policy, 118–134
Foreign trade, 130–131
France (see also De Gaulle), 8, 10, 12, 88, 89
Frankel, H., 147
Frankowski, J., 90, 93

Galbraith, J. K., 102
Galter, A., 95
Gamarnikov, Michael, 79
Germany (West and East) 1, 2, 4, 5, 6, 8,
12, 13, 20, 69, 76, 98, 118, 119, 120, 121, 122, 123, 126, 127, 128, 129, 131, 132, 133
Gesing, R., 29, 58
Gibney, F., 145, 148
Gidyński, J. C., 47
Gierek, Edward, 21, 26, 30, 40, 51, 52–53, 55, 56, 63, 64, 72, 76, 93, 103, 114, 116, 123, 134, 139, 140
GL (People's Guard): see AL (People's Army)
Gomułka, Władysław 14, 21, 24, 26, 27, 28, 30, 33, 37, 39, 40, 48, 49, 50–51, 55, 60, 61, 63, 64–66, 69, 71, 72, 73, 74, 75–76, 78, 82, 83, 87, 93, 98, 101, 106, 109, 110, 116, 117, 119, 120, 122, 123, 124, 125, 126, 127, 128, 129, 130, 132, 134, 135, 136, 137, 138, 139
Gontarz, Ryszard, 77
Government, 25–47
Great Britain, 8, 12, 68, 106, 107
Greece, 131
Groth, A. J., 22, 23, 117, 145
Grynberg, Henryk, 74
Grzybowski, K., 47, 135, 148, 149
Gsovski, V., 47, 95, 148
Gucwa, C., 58
Gwóźdź, J., 78

Hagmayer, Jerzy, 93
Halasz, N., 134
Halecki, Oskar, 21, 147, 148
Hallstein Doctrine, 132
Healey, D., 78
Hiscocks, Richard, 23, 78, 148
Horak, Stephen, 22, 147
Hrynkiewicz, J., 29
Hungary, 61, 63, 76, 118, 120, 121, 123, 125, 133

Ignar, Stanisław, 29
Intellectuals, 62–63, 66–68, 70–71
Israel, 74, 106
Italy, 107

Jabłoński, Henryk, 29
Jadwiga, Queen, 3
Jagiełło, Władysław, King, 3
Jagielski, Mieczysław, 29, 55
Jaroszewicz, Piotr, 29, 40, 55, 76, 77, 94, 140
Jaruzelski, Wojciech, 55, 75, 78
Jaszczuk, Bolesław, 51, 55
Jews: see Anti-semitism

Jędrychowski, Stefan, 15, 30, 55
John XXIII, 88
Jóźwiak, Witold, 63
Judiciary: see Courts, Police and Prosecutor General

Kaczmarek, Bishop, 82, 84
Kadar, Janos, 116
Kaganovich, Lazar, 64
Katyń massacre, 13, 14
Katz-Suchy, J., 75
Kennedy, R. F., 130
Khrushchev, N. S., 62, 64, 72, 125, 129, 132,
Kępa, Józef, 78
Kiesinger, Kurt, 127
Kilaja, J., 47
Kisielewski, S., 77
Kliszko, Zenon, 51, 55, 60, 72
Kłosiewicz, W., 78
Korbel, J., 147, 23
Koćiołek, S., 55
Kohn, Hans, 22
Kolakowski, Leszek, 68, 71
Komarnicki, T., 22
Korboński, A., 78, 117
Korboński, S., 47, 148
Korneychuk, A., 15
Kościuszko, Tadeusz, 6, 7,
Kosygin, Aleksei, 129, 130
Kraśko, Wincenty, 77
KRN (National Home Council), 15
Kruczek, Władysław, 55, 56, 76, 78
Kuhn, D., 95
Kuhn, F., 95
Kulcyzyński, S., 31, 58
Kulski, W. W., 149
Kuroń, Jacek, 71, 75
Kurowski, S., 39

Labedz, L., 79, 117
Land reforms, 96–97
Lange, Oskar, 39, 116
Latin America, 131
Lechowicz, W., 30, 58
Lewiński, P., 29
Lipiński, Edward, 39
Lipset, S. M., 115
Lithuania, 3
Local government: see People's Councils
Loga-Sowiński, Ignacy, 27, 31, 51, 55, 56, 60, 76

Machray, Robert, 23
Mac Eoin, G., 95

Malenkov, G., 62
Mao Tse Tung, 124–125
Marshall Plan, 119
Mazur, F., 63
Marx, Karl, 69
Meyer, A. G., 145
Mickiewicz, Adam, 7
Mieczkowski, B., 117
Mieszko, Duke, 3
Mijał, Kazimierz, 72, 132
Mikołajczyk, Stanisław, 18, 19, 23, 31, 47, 57, 148
Mikoyan, A., 64
Miłosz, Czesław, 68, 148
Minc, Hilary, 15, 48, 69, 72
Misiaszek, Stanisław, 78
Mitręga, J., 29
Moczar, Mieczysław, 9, 30, 55, 69–70, 71, 72, 73, 74, 76, 77, 92, 93, 134, 136, 143, 144
Modzelewski, Karol, 71, 75
Molotov, V. M., 62, 64
Molotov-Ribbentrop Pact, 12, 13
Mond, J., 145
Montias, J. M., 47, 116
Monticone, R. C., 95
Morrison, J. F., 22, 148
Mościcki, Ignacy, 11
Moskwa, Zygmunt, 29, 58
Motyka, L., 29

Nagy, Imre, 124, 125
Nationalism, 7–10, 69–70, 143
Natolin group (see also Stalinism), 63–64
New Zealand, 131
Nixon, Richard M., 130
Nobility (Szlachta), 5–6
North Atlantic Treaty Organization (NATO), 120, 123, 127, 128, 130
Novotny, A., 133
Nowak, J., 145
Nowak, Zenon, 29, 63, 72
NSZ (Nationalist Armed Forces), 61

Ochab, Edward, 31, 62, 63, 70
Oder-Neisse Frontier, 2, 17, 60, 81, 88, 94, 97, 119, 122, 124, 126, 128, 129, 133
Olewiński, Marian, 30
Olszewski, H., 47
Olszowski, Stanisław, 77, 78
Ozga-Michalski, J., 58
OZN (Camp of National Unity), 11, 12
Osóbka-Morawski, Edward, 15, 19

Pakistan, 131
Pan-Germanism, 91
Pasternak, L., 63
Paul VI, 88
Pax, 57, 90–93
Pełczyński, Z. A., 47
Penzik, I., 145
People's Councils, 37–39
Piasecki, Bolesław, 66, 70, 71, 73, 76, 90–94, 143
Piłsudski, Józef, 8, 10, 11, 22, 41
Pisuła, F., 29
Pius XII, 88
Planning, 39, 110–111, 115–116
Pluralism, 136–137
PKWN (Polish Committee of National Liberation), 15
Pobóg-Malinowski, W., 21
Podedworny, B., 31, 58
Police, 19, 45–46, 62, 65–66, 73
Popławski, J. L., 7
Portugal, 131
Poznań (1956) riots, 63
Prosecutor General, 45–46
Przybyła, J., 117
Public opinion, 140–142
Pułaski, Kazimierz, 6
PZPR (United Polish Workers Party): see Communist Party

Radkiewicz, Stanisław, 15, 46, 48, 69
Radliński, A., 29
Rajk, Laszlo, 61
Ranney, A., 47
Rapacki, Adam, 29, 63, 129
Reforms: under Gomułka, 64–67
    under Gierek, 40–41, 76–78, 116, 139–140
Revisionism, 66–69, 143–144
Revolutions: against Russian rule, 7
Richter, R., 145
Rokossovsky, Marshal K., 62, 63, 69, 72
Romkowski, R., 46
Roos, H., 147
Roosevelt, F. D., 16
Rosa, R. A., 47
Rosada, S., 78
Rose, W. J., 23
Rothschild, Joseph, 23, 147
Różanski, S., 46, 72
Rozek, Edward J., 23, 148
Rozental, A. A., 116
Rudziński, A. W., 47
Rumania, 120, 121, 123, 132, 133, 134, 144

Rumiński, Bolesław, 78
Rydz-Śmigły, Edward, 11

Schaff, Adam, 55, 67–68
Schneiderman, S. L., 79, 111
SD (Democratic Party), 58
Segal, S., 22
Seidler, G. L., 47
Sejm, 26–27, 28, 30–31, 32, 36–37
Seton-Watson, H., 24
Sharp, S. L., 78
Shuster, G. N., 95
Schutz, K., 122
Siekanowicz, Piotr, 42
Sikorski, Władysław, 13, 61
Skilling, H. G., 79, 145, 149
Skrzypek, S., 116
Slansky, Rudolf, 61
Sławoj-Składkowski, F., 11
Słonimski, Antoni, 77
Smoliński, Leon, 117
Snyder, L. L., 22
Sobieski, Jan, 3
Social policies, 102–103, 111–115
South Africa, 68
Soviet Union (also USSR and Russia), 1, 2, 4, 5, 7, 8, 12, 13, 16, 18, 20, 25, 26, 49, 50, 61, 62, 63, 64, 65, 67, 74, 76, 87, 88, 97, 99, 104, 115, 118, 120, 121, 122, 123, 124, 125, 126, 128, 129, 130, 131, 132, 133, 134, 141, 142, 144.
Spain, 131
Spychalski, Marian, 27, 29, 51, 55, 60, 75
Sroka, S., 30
Staar, Richard F., 59, 78, 148
Stalin, J. V., 13, 18, 23, 61, 116
Stalinism, 19, 49–50, 63–64, 71–72, 77–78
Staniewicz, W., 116
Stankiewicz, W. J., 116
Stawiński, E., 29
Stehle, Hansjakob, 47, 78, 148
Stern, P. H., 24
Stowe, L., 78
Stroński, Stanisław, 78
Strzelecki, Ryszard, 55, 70
Students, 71, 73, 75, 104–105, 111–112
Światło, Józef, 47
Świtała, Franciszek, 76
Symmons-Symonolewicz, K., 21
Syrop, Konrad, 78, 148
Szaz, Z. M., 21
Szlachćic, Franciszek, 70, 78
Sznajder, E., 29

Sztachelski, J., 30
Szydlak, Jan, 55
Szyr, Eugeniusz, 29, 72

Tejchma, Józef, 55
Terror: see Police
"Thaw", 62–63
Tito, J. (see also Titoism and Yugoslavia),
    61, 116, 120, 124, 125
Titoism, 61
Tobias, R., 95
Trade Unions, 56–57, 78
Trąmpczyński, Witold, 29
Tucker, R. C., 145
Twentieth Congress of the CPSU, 62
Tykociński, W., 135

Ukraine, 2, 8, 9, 11, 20
Ulam, Adam, 78
Union of Polish Patriots, 15
United Nations, 97, 119, 129
United States, 8, 68, 82, 97, 106, 107,
    116, 119, 126, 131

Vatican, 88, 91, 94
Verba, S., 22
Versailles Conference, 8
Vietnam, 35

Wade, L. L., 117
Wagner, W., 21
Walczac, Stanisław, 29
Wandycz, Piotr S., 135, 147
Waniołka, F., 29
Wańkowicz, M., 71
Warsaw Pact, 120, 123
Warsaw Uprising, 16
Wasilewska, Wanda, 15

Wellisz, S., 135
Ważyk, Adam, 63, 66
Wende, J. K., 58
Wiatr, J. J., 34, 35, 47
Wilson, Woodrow, 8
Winston, V., 135
Witos, Wincenty, 22
Władysław IV, 5
Wójcicka, Janina, 105, 111
Wojtyla, Karol, Cardinal, 88
Wszelaki, J., 135
Woods, W., 148
Workers' Councils and Conferences of
    Worker-Self-Government, 39–41
World War II, consequences in Poland,
    2–3, 12, 98,
Wycech, Czesław, 57
Wyszyński, Stefan, Cardinal, 66, 77, 81,
    82, 83, 84, 85, 86, 87, 88, 94

Yakubovsky, I. I., 121
Yalta Conference, 18
Yugoslavia (see also Tito and Titoism),
    124, 125, 131, 132, 134, 144

Zambrowski, Roman, 63, 72
Zamoyski, Maurycy, 113
Zauberman, A., 148
Zawadzki, Alexander, 15, 63
Zawieyski, Jerzy, 27, 75, 89
Zawodny, J. K., 23
Zinner, Paul E., 23, 47, 79
ZMS (Association of Socialist Youth), 40
ZMW (Association of Rural Youth), 40
ZSL (United Peasant Party), 57–58
Znak, 89, 90
Żukowski, S., 117
Żyzniewski, S. J., 135